WHEN DO YOU KNOW THE
HONEYMOON
IS
OVER?

2012.

Lolo,
Mary Christmas
I hope you never find
out the answer to this
question! Love, Peg

WHEN DO YOU KNOW THE
HONEYMOON
IS
OVER?

APANDISIS
α
PUBLISHING

Apandisis Publishing
105 Madison Avenue, Suite 3A
New York, New York 10016

ISBN-13: 978-1-4127-5275-6
ISBN-10: 1-4127-5275-2

Manufactured in USA

8 7 6 5 4 3 2 1

www.FYIanswers.com

Contents

Chapter Three
WEIRD SCIENCE AND TECHNOLOGY

Chapter Four
FOOD AND DRINK

Chapter Five
ANIMAL KINGDOM

Chapter Six
BODY SCIENCE

Chapter Seven
TRADITIONS

Chapter Eight
EARTH AND SPACE

Chapter Nine
SPORTS

Chapter Ten
PLACES

Chapter Eleven
HEALTH MATTERS

Chapter Fourteen
MORE GOOD STUFF

Chapter One

LOVE AND LUST

Q When do you know the honeymoon is over?

A When she stops waxing her fuzzy upper lip? When he starts living in a Jimmy Buffet T-shirt he bought in 1982? When the two of you quit kissing, groping, and goo-gooing all over each other in broad daylight on community property?

The truth is, there isn't a set time limit for the honeymoon phase of a relationship. It can last anywhere from five minutes to five years. But this much is certain: There is no way any couple can sustain its initial level of attraction, emotion, and passion for the entire long haul.

Relationship experts say that the average honeymoon phase lasts from six months to two years. During this time, you prepare for each and every date like it's a job interview. Every hair is in place, teeth are flossed, the toilet is scrubbed. He treats her like a brand new car; she sees him as that elusive pair of perfectly fitting jeans. Elizabeth Ritzman, a clinical professional counselor, says that the honeymoon stage is "a wonderful time during the relationship when we try to present our best selves to new lovers whom we tend to idealize and who idealize us. Serious relational conflict is avoided."

When does the honeymoon phase start moving closer to that more mundane edge of reality? Probably right around the time your pen hits the paper. Soon after you co-sign the marriage license or co-lease a new apartment, you know the thrill is just about to dissipate. There's no more playing cat and mouse. The deal is sealed. The eagle has landed. The hunter has been hunted. Game over.

And what a relief! You can finally quit maintaining the façade and just be yourself. After spending all of these months together, you have settled into a daily routine. You have found your niche, your comfort zone. By now, you are so familiar with each other that you can complete each other's sentences—and even pee with the bathroom door open. And yet his incessant snoring is really beginning to annoy you. And she spent how much on that designer handbag?

Suddenly, it hits you: Is this what the relationship is all about? What happened to the flowers, the fireworks, the six-pack abs? Why are there always dishes piled up in the sink? Why doesn't she cook my favorite pot roast for dinner anymore?

You can only gloss over your differences and disappointments for so long. As Everett L. Worthington Jr. explains in his book *Marriage Counseling*, during the honeymoon phase "each person feels a little upset that things are not being done 'correctly.'" Inevitably, tension mounts. And that first major disagreement usually comes when one mate isn't living up to the other's expectations.

So you see, she's really not a domestic goddess who turns out home-baked apple turnovers every Sunday morning. And no, he's not a clean-cut neat freak who never, ever stinks up the bathroom. As a wise man once said: "When the honeymoon is over, a man discovers his wife isn't an angel, so he quits posing as a saint."

Q Why do women need so many shoes?

A Where's Imelda Marcos when you need her? The former first lady of the Philippines—and world's best-known shoe collector—reportedly owned 1,220 pairs when she fled the presidential palace in 1986. She would be the perfect source for a definitive answer to this age-old question, but alas, she's probably out prancing through the streets of Manila in expensive size eight-and-a-half Ferragamos.

So instead, let's address why men find this footwear fixation so perplexing in the first place. Minus the few who engage in cross-dressing, men are generally wearing pants, or some variation thereof. Said pants come in three basic colors: black, navy, and khaki.

You know what that means? No one is going to crane his or her neck to see what Joe is sporting underneath his spiffy cuffed-hem Dockers. And it doesn't matter anyway. Chances are that Joe's shoes are typical leather loafers or lace-up oxfords, in a pedestrian shade of black or brown. The heels are unremarkably flat, unless Joe happens to be living in seventeenth-century France or competing in a professional ballroom dancing competition.

Most guys can get by with five pairs of shoes or fewer. These include—and are often limited to—dress shoes for work, athletic shoes for working out, and a pair of scuffs for picking up the Sunday paper. And this is exactly why men don't get why women need so many shoes—the operative word being "need."

You see, modern women are major multitaskers. Shoes take their scurrying feet to work, the gym, day care, the grocery store, the beach, after-school sports, dancing, and swanky dinner parties— all in the span of a week. Yes, it's true that you can wear only one pair of shoes at a time. But if you've ever had a stiletto heel get caught in a muddy sinkhole of damp grass, you know that you simply cannot wear a pair of four-inch Jimmy Choos to the park.

Take a look in a woman's closet and you'll find pants, skirts, shorts, skorts, and dresses of every conceivable color and length. Most of these fashions direct an observer's eye right to a woman's legs and feet—so guess what? The style, heel, and color of her shoes have to be spot-on.

Shoe designers know this, and that's why you find women's shoes with wedge heels, kitten heels, peep toes, Mary Jane straps, and colors like orange patent leather. And it's a good thing, because the busy women of this world clearly need shoes for every outfit, every occasion, and every terrain.

The truth? Men just can't handle that amount of mind-blowing fashion coordination. If they could, they'd be smart enough to own more than one pair of Nikes.

Q Is going to a strip club or viewing Internet porn considered cheating?

A It all depends on the code of conduct that has been established by the couple in question.

Let's start with strip clubs. If a wife tells her husband (or vice versa) that strip clubs are off-limits, but he ignores her and goes anyway, he's a cheater. But if the two agree that it's okay to look but not touch, going to a strip club is fine. Some partners even encourage it: Such visits might heighten the patron's sexual energy, which can be converted into increased verve in the couple's own bedroom upon his or her return. Of course, the "look but don't touch" element is the key to the whole deal—if the husband heads off to a strip club and gets a lap dance in the champagne room, the line starts to become awfully blurry.

Internet porn can be an even more slippery slope. Some varieties of Internet porn are as innocuous as the pages of a pin-up calendar, but the stakes escalate in a hurry. For example, there are sites on which you can enjoy a virtual visit via a one-way Web cam with a willing—and often naked—partner. The "next level" of Internet porn involves chat rooms and instant messaging, which allow for a certain amount of intimacy with another individual. Sure, it may all be make-believe, but this type of emotional role-playing can be harmful to a marriage.

Some couples view Internet porn together in order to get in the mood. This, of course, isn't cheating. But as with strip clubs, the line can easily become blurred. If you and your spouse enjoy perusing porn on the Web—either separately or together—make sure to set clear boundaries. Otherwise, trouble may start brewing on the home front.

As you can see, there aren't cut-and-dried rules when it comes to strip clubs and Internet porn. What some couples call cheating, others call foreplay.

Q Is chocolate an aphrodisiac?

A This question has been debated for ages. Giacomo Casanova—the poster boy for carnal exploration—certainly thought that chocolate did the trick. The eighteenth-century Italian would drink the sweet stuff before embarking on his amorous adventures.

Modern-day scientists are less convinced that chocolate is an aphrodisiac, although many do concede that the confection contains some curious properties. They're found in chocolate's key ingredient, the cacao bean, and include:

- Phenylethylamine (PEA). PEA causes blood pressure and blood-sugar levels to rise, temporarily resulting in heightened alertness and a state of happiness.
- Caffeine. This strong, fast-acting stimulant increases the heart rate and gets the blood flowing to all the right places.
- Anandamide. A type of cannabinoid—yes, cannabinoids are also found in marijuana—anandamide produces feelings of contentment.
- Theobromine. This mild, long-lasting stimulant has a mood-lifting effect. It opens blood vessels and stimulates heart muscle tissue.
- Tryptophan. Tryptophan triggers a discharge of serotonin, which provides an overall sense of happiness.

In addition, the consumption of chocolate prompts the body to release endorphins. What's so great about endorphins? Plenty: They are natural opiates that lower a person's sensitivity to pain and deliver feelings of contentment.

So, yes, chocolate can make you happy, happy, happy. But does it enhance sexual desire? That's the million-dollar question—and no one's come up with a definitive answer. John Renner, the founder of the Consumer Health Information Research Institute, has an intriguing take on the matter: "The mind is the most potent aphrodisiac there is. It's very difficult to evaluate something someone is taking because if you tell them it's an aphrodisiac, the hope of a certain response might actually lead to an additional sexual reaction."

In other words, the biggest thing chocolate has going for it on the love front is its reputation. Chocolate helped to turn the great Casanova into a sex machine, so why shouldn't it do the same for Ed from Pittsburgh? It's basically the placebo effect: If you think chocolate will get you in the mood, then it will get you in the mood.

Of course, many people eat chocolate simply for the pleasurable taste—and that's okay, too. Whether consumed right out of the wrapper or melted and poured over your lover's privates before being devoured, chocolate packs a powerful punch.

Q How did Xs and Os become shorthand for hugs and kisses?

A Are you one of those people who signs letters with cutesy Xs and Os to indicate hugs and kisses? Did you ever stop to wonder why you're doing that? What is so cuddly about an X or an O? Much like love itself, the how and why of it remain matters of conjecture.

The X can be traced as far back as the tenth century BC, when it was used as the Paleo–Hebrew letter *Tav* and the symbol of the seal of Hashem (God), which stood for truth, completeness, and perfection. During the early Christian era, the X character signified the cross of Calvary (the Latin cross mounted on three steps) and was the first letter in Christ's name (Xristos).

Fast-forward to the Middle Ages, when illiterate people supposedly substituted an X for their signatures. They would then kiss the mark, an act that was comparable to kissing a crucifix or Bible and implied a sworn oath. This practice continued until as recently as one hundred and fifty years ago.

According to the *Oxford English Dictionary,* the earliest known use of an X to signify a kiss was in 1763. However, this date is debatable—the practice may have started with handwritten notes, so documentation may be incomplete, which makes it difficult for lexicographers to pin down exact dates and sources.

For our purposes, the origins of the O are even more elusive. In his book *The Joys of Yiddish,* author Leo Rosten wrote that Jewish immigrants in the United States chose an O as their signature, as opposed to a cross symbol that represented Christ. Shopkeepers and salespeople also purportedly signed receipts using an O. Of course, this explanation does little to solve the hugs-and-kisses riddle.

There is even a running debate about which letter represents hugs and which represents kisses. If you look closely, you will see that the outline of an X can suggest a silhouette of the union of two pairs of lips. Dear Uncle Ezra, an online question-and-answer forum from Cornell University, posits that the X resembles a single pair of lips pursing for a kiss. Some researchers contend that the X implies a hug because it resembles two pairs of crisscrossing arms. On the other hand, the O could be the hug, as it might represent a pair of arms encircling another person. Or it could be the kiss-use your imagination and you'll see the pouty imprint of a smooch.

Whatever the particulars, Xs and Os should continue to flourish in this era of shorthand text messaging. Unless they are elbowed out by LOL ("lots of love"), of course. To that unthinkable possibility, we say, OMG ("oh my god").

Q Is the woman who catches the bridal bouquet always the next one to get married?

A The institution of marriage is nearly as old as civilization itself, so it's natural that plenty of wedding-day superstitions have evolved over the years. It seems that much needs to be done in order to ensure enduring love, healthy children, and prosperity. Among other acts, the bride and groom exchange rings (as symbols of their everlasting union), have rice thrown at them (to bring about fertility and prosperity), and dig into a massive, ornate cake (more fertility mojo, with some general good luck sprinkled in).

For a woman to even reach the wedding altar—at least expeditiously—another superstition comes into play: She must catch a bride's bouquet. This one has its origins in fourteenth-century France, where the garter—which was thought to bring good luck—was tossed to wedding guests by the bride. In the next century, tossing the garter got tossed out the window, and brides started throwing their stockings to onlookers.

But taking one's stockings off in the midst of a party sometimes proved to be embarrassing, so during the mid-fifteenth century, one bright-minded bride thought to give her bouquet a toss instead. A tradition was born. In England, wedding guests who desired to share in the bride's happiness wanted "a piece of her"; the bride would throw her bouquet to placate them. Somewhere along the way (it's not known exactly when), catching the bouquet brought more than luck—it became a quick ticket to marriage. Or so the myth goes. There isn't a shred of legitimate evidence that the woman who catches the bridal bouquet will be the next to get married.

This might actually be good news for potential bouquet-catchers. Nearly half of marriages today end in divorce—the institution seems to have become about as disposable as a love note. Dreams of happily-ever-after have been supplanted by a whirlwind wedding, a head-spinning honeymoon, and a quickie divorce.

So do you want to tempt the fates, as unsubstantiated as they may be, and try to catch that bouquet? Go ahead. We dare you.

Q Should a woman have sex on a first date?

A Before answering this doozy of a question, we need to take a close look at that first date. There are many possible outcomes, and—sorry, guys—they don't all involve sex.

Here's a sampling: If the woman never wants to see the man again because there is clearly no chemistry between them and he's a jerk, then an end-of-the-night hookup is pretty much out of the question. If the guy's a bit of a jerk but there is some chemistry, the potential for a one-night stand exists. If the woman is in the market for a FWB (friend with benefits), sex on the first "date" is a possibility. Or if the woman senses that she might want a long-term relationship with the man, she'll probably want to protect her virtue on their first night out together.

The scenarios seem endless, but here's a good rule of thumb for a woman who's on a date with a man she just met: Don't have sex with him. (Sorry again, guys.) He may wind up being someone who's significantly less worthy than Prince Charming, so it's better to be safe than sorry.

Some words for the wary: A woman needs to be careful to protect her identity—in other words, she shouldn't give a man she barely knows her phone numbers, address, or any other personal information. The first date should take place in a public setting—not at the guy's bachelor's pad—and the woman should watch her drink at all times to ensure that it doesn't get spiked with something harmful, such as a date-rape drug. Finally, she should let a friend know where she plans to meet up with the man.

So, ladies, it's always wise to err on the side of caution on a first date. As for the second, third, or fourth date? If you've ascertained that the man's aim is true, and you're in the mood, have at it.

Q Why is kissing such a turn on?

A Close your eyes and imagine you're with someone who really does it for you. Your lips are pressed against his or hers, the person's tongue is touching yours, and you can feel his or her warm, heavy breaths on your cheek. These sensations are enough to make your body tingle, and the sexual energy builds.

Need we say more? When two people are "swapping spit," it's generally because they're hot for each other. So a rush factor is involved—in fact, kissing can cause such a rush that it's possible to achieve an adrenaline high. And when your body releases adrenaline, your brain unleashes the "feel good" chemicals dopamine, phenylethylamine (PEA), and norepinephrine. As the excitement heightens, your body also begins to release endorphins, which work as natural opiates.

All of this adds up to powerful feelings of warmth and intimacy. You may even get a sense of lightheadedness—it's not uncommon for people to speak of being woozy or "weak in the knees" after a make-out session with that special someone. Other effects that are associated with deep, passionate kissing include increased cardiovascular activity and oxygenation of the blood. This helps explain why some fitness trainers recommend kissing as a way of burning excess calories and getting in some cardio.

Sex experts say that kissing is one of the best ways to engage in foreplay. In addition to providing pleasure in itself, kissing can be a catalyst for deeper erotic interactions because it allows for a greater blood flow to the erogenous zones of the body. A kiss, it seems, is a lot more than the swapping of spit—it can be a gateway to paradise.

Q Why is baseball such a common metaphor for sex?

A This question makes us hark back wistfully to high school: the cool guy bragging about getting to third base with his girlfriend; the geek complaining that his homecoming date wouldn't let him get to first base. It seems we'd almost be unable to talk about sex without baseball. What is it about the sport that lends itself to such metaphorical flourishes?

Its long history, for starters. Baseball is woven into the fabric of American culture, and most people understand how the game works. A cricket metaphor, for example, just wouldn't resonate the same way with Americans, although "wicket" has some delightful possibilities. But there's more to it than that. A baseball bat is about as obvious a phallic symbol as you can find in the world of sports; combine it with balls, and you have metaphorical magic. Furthermore, the progression of the runner around the bases easily translates to the sexual sphere.

For those of you who had your faces in books while your fellow students had their faces, er, elsewhere, what follows is a quick summary of the baserunning/sex analogy. Typically, "first base" is the kissing stage. This metaphor, according to the *Random House Historical Dictionary of American Slang,* dates back to 1928. "Second base" is fondling, or what used to be called "petting." "Third base" is either oral sex or mutual masturbation (which works nicely because a triple in baseball is the rarest of hits). And a "home run" means going all the way.

Other sex-related terms are also drawn from baseball, such as "striking out" (which some of us know all too well), "switch-hitter" (which refers to a bisexual), and "pitcher" and "catcher" (the designations for active and passive partners, respectively, in a homosexual relationship). No, you just can't beat fun at the old ballpark.

Q Why is the area where prostitutes work called a red-light district?

A The first printed mention of a red-light district was made in 1894 in a Milwaukee newspaper, the *Sentinel,* but the semantic origin of the term is open to debate.

One explanation, which dates back to about the time of the *Sentinel*'s article, relates to the red lanterns that railroad workers took with them into town when they had time off during a trip. The lanterns were kept lit so that the crew could be rounded up quickly if needed. If the men were engaging prostitutes, who tended to cluster in one section of town, that area was marked by many red lanterns. Others suggest that the term refers to the red shades that prostitutes of the early twentieth century put over candles and lamps as a discrete signal to passersby of their services.

The color red has long been connected to prostitution. Red paper lanterns were placed outside brothels in ancient China, and in the Biblical story of Rahab, a house of ill-repute was indicated with a red rope. During World War I, red lights in Belgian brothels indicated that the available services were for non-officers. (Brothels for officers sported blue lights.)

Color theorists—scholars who study the effects and meanings of colors to humans and animals across time and geographical boundaries—widely note that red is associated with sensual matters. In the United States, the color red has long been associated with the concepts of "stop" and "love." And aren't the women who work in a red-light district just trying to get men to stop and love?

Q Why is rice tossed after a wedding?

A If you think about it, throwing something at the bride and groom after a wedding ceremony to ensure fertility is downright odd, but it's been going on for centuries. As with seemingly every tradition, this one might date back to ancient Rome, where wheat was the grain of choice.

This custom was also practiced in Asia, where throwing rice meant "may you always have a full pantry." In England, wheat was thrown at the newlyweds until folks decided to get fancy—they baked the wheat grains into small cakes that were crumbled over the bride's head. Unfortunately (or not), the wheat cakes were so wonderful that it seemed a shame not to eat them. So the tradition became one in which the wheat cake was eaten by the bride, and guests threw grain. Rice was preferred for throwing because it was less expensive than wheat.

This isn't to say that rice is the only way to go. Moroccans throw figs and dates in the hopes that the marriage will be, well, fruitful. In Korea, the groom's parents pelt their new daughter-in-law with dates and chestnuts to ensure grandchildren. In some European countries, brides and grooms get hit with eggs, and at traditional Irish weddings, brides and grooms are pelted with pots and pans. Ouch!

In 1996, legendary advice columnist Ann Landers urged her readers not to throw rice at weddings. She claimed that birds eat the uncooked rice, which expands in their stomachs and causes them to explode. Although the USA Rice Federation quickly issued a news release asking Landers to "straighten up and fly right when you talk about birds," there has been a considerable movement to instead throw birdseed, flower petals, or mini-marshmallows at the newlyweds.

It's a needless break from tradition. After all, there are no record-ed reports of birds exploding at wedding venues.

Q Do menopausal women lose their sex drive?

A Of course they do. Just take apart the word phonetically: men-o-pause. It says so right there: a pause from men.

Our lame attempt at humor may strike a nerve, especially in the typically cranky women who are experiencing the onset of meno-pause. On a more serious note, we need to provide definitions of "sex drive" and "menopause" before answering this question.

A person's sex drive is called the libido, which is a physical and mental urge to partake in sexual activities. Note that this means more than actually having sex: It is the *desire* for sex—the ability to fantasize about it, to yearn for it, and even to miss it.

Menopause can be described as the end of the fertile stage of a woman's life. It typically begins between the ages of forty-five and fifty-five and means that she no longer has a menstrual cycle and can no longer bear children.

Many of the mood swings and changes in body temperature and tastes that beset menopausal women can be linked directly to their hormones. Hormones are the chemicals that keep a body in sync; when our hormone levels change, we don't feel like ourselves. A primary hormone that is involved in a woman's libido is estrogen, and its levels nose-dive during menopause. This decrease of estrogen commonly causes symptoms such as vaginal atrophy and dehydration.

These symptoms can make sex painful for women; thus, a roll in the hay is something that they may try to avoid. Decreases in the levels of the hormones progesterone and testosterone can also have an adverse effect on a woman's sex drive—progesterone keeps the libido humming, and testosterone also spurs sexual desire and lubricates the vagina.

Nevertheless, it's not all doom and gloom in the bedroom: Only 20 to 45 percent of menopausal women report diminished sex drives. So despite the dramatic changes that are occurring in their bodies, many women still think about, and engage in, sex.

Chapter Two

PEOPLE

Q Who's Oscar, and why is he associated with an Academy Award?

A Oscar de la Renta. Oscar Madison. Oscar the Grouch. Famous Oscars all, but perhaps none is more recognizable than the 13.5-inch statuette that is handed out at the annual Academy Awards ceremony. Who is this golden boy, anyway?

Oscar looks like your everyday nude dude (albeit non-anatomically correct), but he's actually a knight. He holds a crusader's sword and stands upon a film reel that has five spokes that represent the original branches of the Academy of Motion Picture Arts and Sciences: actors, writers, directors, producers, and technicians.

Why is he called Oscar instead of something befitting a knight, maybe Arthur or Geoffrey or Tristan? The question has sparked debate in Hollywood and beyond. One widely believed—though unsubstantiated—explanation is that the handle originated with former academy librarian Margaret Herrick. Around 1931, she is supposed to have commented that the statuette bore an uncanny resemblance to her uncle, a Texas farmer named Oscar Pierce (actually he was her cousin).

Another popular answer involves legendary actress Bette Davis. She is said to have named the Best Actress Academy Award she won in 1936 for her performance in *Dangerous* after her ex-husband, bandleader Harmon Oscar Nelson Jr. Apparently, Davis thought the, um, backsides of Oscar the statuette and Oscar the bandleader were similarly shaped.

However the moniker came to be, it caught on quickly. The academy officially adopted it as the statuette's nickname in 1939, and few people today would know Oscar by his formal title: The Academy Award of Merit.

Q Who shot whom at the O.K. Corral?

A First, the famous showdown in Tombstone, Arizona, didn't take place in the O.K. Corral. It happened in the city's vacant lot No. 2. Somehow, "The Shoot-Out in Vacant Lot No. 2" doesn't have quite the same ring to it, so a savvy journalist or scriptwriter must have moved the action a few yards over.

Second, despite what the movies may suggest, it wasn't a simple tale of white hats versus black hats. The real story has as many twists and turns as a warren of prairie dog tunnels, with a round-up of suspects that includes carousing cowboys, contentious lawmen, corrupt politicians, card sharks, cattle rustlers, a dentist named Doc, and Doc's lady friend (the appropriately named Big Nose Kate).

What do we know for sure? On October 26, 1881, at around 3:00 PM, four men entered the lot behind the O.K. Corral: Wyatt  Earp; his brothers, Virgil and Morgan; and John Henry "Doc" Holliday. There, they encountered Ike Clanton, his brother Billy, Frank and Tom McLaury, and Billy Claiborne. Thirty seconds later, both of the McLaury brothers and Billy Clanton were dead. Virgil and Morgan Earp sustained serious wounds, Holliday suffered a minor injury, and Wyatt walked out without a scratch.

What brought them there? Trouble had been brewing between the Earp and Clanton factions for some time. Doc Holliday, a Philadelphia-trained dentist, preferred playing cards to pulling teeth, and this habit often left him short of cash. Earlier in 1881, he had been accused of stagecoach robbery by his own girl-friend, Big Nose Kate. The Earp brothers suspected that Ike Clanton had put her up to it to deflect suspicion from his own friends. When four of those friends turned up dead, Clanton accused the Earps, and the bad blood began to boil.

Who fired first? Most historians agree that Holliday and Morgan Earp started it, one wounding Frank McLaury and the other Billy Clanton. With that, as the locals say, "the ball had begun." An estimated thirty shots were fired within half a minute. Wyatt claimed that seventeen were his, though he is only thought to have killed one man, Tom McLaury.

The Earps and Holliday were ultimately acquitted of any wrong-doing. Several months later, Morgan Earp was shot to death by unknown assailants. Wyatt spent the next two years tracking down anyone he thought was connected with his brother's death. Was he "brave, courageous, and bold," as the song says? Or was he just a ruthless vigilante? The jury is still out. One thing is certain, though: Wyatt Earp was an American original, and his story will be told for generations to come.

Q Can women serve on U.S. submarines?

A Women can fly multimillion-dollar fighter jets off the decks of aircraft carriers, but when it comes to steering a sardine can through water, they're out of luck. So says the U.S. Navy, which has integrated women into almost every level of service—but not on submarines.

Why? Consider the obvious: Submarines are tiny. About 140 crew members are crammed—like sardines, if you will—into a submarine that might be just 377 feet long. With passageways so narrow that sailors are often forced to turn sideways to pass by each other, and bunk space so limited that crew members must sleep in shifts, submarines force shipmates into quarters so tight that co-ed life would feature plenty of awkward situations.

Higher-ups in the Navy have worried that these cramped conditions, coupled with weeks of complete isolation from the surface world, would naturally encourage amorous relationships, which would, in turn, make for some intense and complicated work situations. And the Navy has long maintained that altering the layout or size of subs to accommodate both genders isn't feasible.

But the tide may be turning. Early in 2008, a U.S. military advisory committee recommended that women be allowed to serve on submarines, an opportunity that had already been granted to women from Australia, Norway, and Sweden. What about the aforementioned obstacles that have so concerned U.S. Navy brass? Simple: The crews would be female-only.

Backed by President George W. Bush, the Navy implemented a plan to build two *Virginia* class nuclear attack subs designed specifically for all-female crews. (It's only a coincidence that the chosen submarine class was indirectly named after that paragon of feminine celibacy and virtue, Elizabeth I, the Virgin Queen.) It's an ingenious solution to a tricky problem.

Q How do you become a saint?

A Everyone who has worked in an office environment has encountered that guy who thinks he should be a saint. You know, the only person who ever fills the copy machine with paper? The benevolent soul—the only one, to hear him tell it—who respects his coworkers enough to clean up after himself in the break room? Yeah, that guy. He should be a saint, right?

With apologies to Bob from Human Resources, becoming a saint is quite a bit more complicated than being punctual for staff meetings. Though most religions throughout history have honored particularly holy members in different ways, most people think of sainthood—at least in Western culture—in terms of Roman Catholicism. In the Catholic church, the process of becoming a saint is known as canonization.

Though sainthood is the ultimate honor in the Catholic church, good Christians who are destined to become saints won't know it during their lifetime—the canonization process starts after the candidate has died. In fact, there usually is a five-year waiting period after death before the Catholic church will consider a candidate for sainthood. Once the waiting period is finished, local church officials will study the life and writings of the proposed saint to make sure that he or she lived a truly Christian life. If the person passes muster, the pope labels him or her "venerable."

The next step in canonization involves attributing a miracle—such as spontaneous healings at the candidate's grave or spontaneous appearances of holy images—to the now-venerable candidate. (Sorry, Bob, but filing your TPS report by deadline doesn't count.) Once the church determines that the miracle in question can be attributed to the candidate, that person is "beatified."

However, beatification still isn't enough to become a saint. Because anyone can get lucky and cure a paraplegic once—look, even a blind squirrel can stumble upon one nut—the church requires a second miracle to ensure that the first wasn't a fluke. Only after this second miracle is confirmed is the candidate officially made a saint.

There is a quicker way to sainthood—martyrdom. So if Bob from HR really wants to become a saint, there are probably plenty of volunteers who would help him along that path.

Q Who in the Sam Hill was Sam Hill?

A Colonel Samuel Hill made a bid for immortality, and depending on how you look at it, he either succeeded in spectacular fashion or failed miserably. His name is certainly remembered—often in times of frustration, bewilderment, and despair—especially if there happens to be a lady present.

"Sam Hill" has been used as a mild expletive, a replacement for "hell" or "damn," since at least the 1830s. The phrase was especially popular among cowboys, who used it in an attempt to clean up their language in mixed company. "Sam Hill" appeared in print for the first time in 1839, in the *Seattle Times* newspaper.

Several stories concerning the origin of this phrase have circulated throughout the years, one of which centers on the aforementioned Colonel Sam Hill, who hailed from Connecticut. Edwin Mitchell's *Encyclopedia of American Politics,* published in 1946, reports that the Colonel ran for political office repeatedly—and failed every time. Thus, to "go like Sam Hill" or to "run like Sam Hill" initially referred to Hill's relentless pursuit of office, even after it became obvious that the public did not want him there. Over time, the term devolved into the more general usage with which we are familiar today.

A simpler explanation is that "hill" was simply a substitute for "hell," in the manner of "heck," based on the similarity of the two words. It has been suggested that the name Sam comes from Samiel, the name given to the devil in Carl Maria von Weber's opera *Der Freischütz*. The opera was performed in New York City in 1825, a little more than a decade before the phrase's first print usage.

Still, for some, the name Sam Hill will always refer to the Colonel. He tried his darnedest to make a place for himself in history and, in failing so many times, succeeded in a way he never could have imagined. No one remembers the man—Mitchell's entry in his *Encyclopedia of American Politics* is essentially the last remaining evidence of his existence—but we all know his name. Problem is, no one knows for sure what the Sam Hill it means.

Q What do Beefeaters have to do with beef... or gin?

A For most tourists, no trip to England is complete without a visit to the Tower of London and a gawk at its festively decorated guards, popularly known as Beefeaters. Many an outsider's knowledge of these venerated guards involves little more than teenage memories of filching a bottle of gin from their parents' liquor cabinet.

Indeed, the picture of the marching soldier on the Beefeater-brand gin label evokes the image of a jovial, beef-munching imbiber—not a bad life, really. So imagine an ignorant tourist's disappointment upon arriving at the Tower of London and finding that the Beefeaters aren't swilling gin and carving up roasts and—worse—prefer not to be called Beefeaters at all.

The so-called Beefeaters are properly known as Yeoman Warders and are assigned to guard the Tower of London and the British crown jewels (which is not a euphemism). Today, their duties are largely ceremonial and they are a popular tourist attraction, but this wasn't always the case.

In 1485, King Henry VII formed a detachment of personal guards, known as Yeomen of the Guard. Shortly thereafter he designated a subgroup, known as Yeoman Warders, to guard the Tower. The Yeoman Warders became jailers and guardsmen of the many famous prisoners who unhappily called the Tower of London home. Over the years, these prisoners included Scottish nationalist William Wallace (who was memorialized in the film *Braveheart*), disfavored queen Anne Boleyn, English conspirator Guy Fawkes, and Nazi officer Rudolf Hess. Some were tortured or executed, and the responsibility for such unsavory tasks fell to the Warders.

Modern Yeoman Warders largely provide tours and ceremonial performances for fanny-pack-wearing tourists—but they are not actors. To be appointed a Yeoman Warder, an applicant must have at least twenty-two years of experience in the British military and must have received service medals and honors. They are congenial, but don't make the mistake of calling them Beefeaters—the nickname was probably first used derisively.

It might have come from the popular belief that Guardsmen were allowed to eat at the king's table and, thus, partake of meals that often featured beef, which commoners could rarely afford in medieval times. It's true that at one time beef made up the bulk of a Yeoman Warder's ration, but according to the *Oxford English Dictionary,* "beefeater" had long been a pejorative term for a menial servant who was fed beef from the master's table.

As for the gin that draws its name from these ceremonial guards, no official sources suggest that the Yeoman Warders must partake. But considering the large number of tourists with whom they have to deal each day, we would imagine that they do.

Q Who invented the brown paper bag?

A Consider the familiar, flat-bottomed brown paper bag: It's useful, ubiquitous, and utterly simple. Now get a sheet of brown paper, a pair of scissors, and some glue, and try to make one yourself. Not so simple, huh?

In 1870, Margaret Knight of the Columbia Paper Bag Company in Springfield, Massachusetts, was doing the same kind of puzzling over paper bags. Back then, the only paper bags that were being manufactured by machine were the narrow, envelope kind, with a single seam at the bottom. Flimsy and easily broken, they were despised by merchants and shoppers alike. The paper bag business was not booming. So Maggie Knight set out to build a better bag.

Born in 1838, Knight had been tinkering with tools since childhood; while other girls played with dolls, she excelled at making sleds and kites. She was especially fascinated by heavy machinery. At the age of twelve, she invented a stop-motion safety device for automatic looms after witnessing an accident in a textile mill that nearly cost a worker his finger. Though never patented, her invention was widely employed throughout the industry.

During her twenties and early thirties, Knight tried her hand at several occupations before finally landing at Columbia Paper Bag. Working alone at night in her boarding house, she designed a machine that could cut, fold, and glue sheets of paper into sturdy, flat-bottomed bags. This time, she applied for a patent. On July 11, 1871, Patent No. 116842 was issued to Margaret E. Knight for a "Bag Machine." Her employer was eager to implement her design, but the male workers he hired to build and install the new machines refused to take direction from a woman, until they were convinced that Maggie was indeed the "mother" of this particular invention.

Knight also had to fend off a challenge to her patent by a rival mechanist, who had spied on the construction of her first prototype. The court decided in her favor, and she persisted in her career. After leaving Columbia, she cofounded the Eastern Paper Bag Company in Hartford, Connecticut, and also supervised her own machine shop in Boston. Between 1871 and 1911, she received twenty-six patents in her own name and is thought to have contributed to more than fifty inventions patented by others; she also built scores of unpatented devices. Upon her death in 1914, the press lauded her as America's "female Edison."

Among her most successful inventions were an easy-to-install window frame, a number-stamping machine, and a mechanical roasting spit. The humble paper bag, however, remains her greatest contribution to civilization. Even today, bag manufacturers rely on her basic concept. So the next time you decide to brown-bag your lunch, stop and give thanks to Maggie Knight for the paper bag—useful, ubiquitous, and a work of genius, too!

Q Who was the real John Henry?

When John Henry was a bitty baby,
Sittin' on his pappy's knee,
He picked up a hammer and a little piece of steel,
And said, "This hammer's gonna be the death of me,
Lord, Lord, this hammer's gonna be the death of me."

A Was it the death of him? Did John Henry, that steel-driving man, really win a contest with a steam drill only to die of exhaustion and a broken heart? There seem to be as many candidates for the real John Henry as there are versions of the song. He was African American or Irish or maybe Polish. He came from West Virginia, Alabama, North Carolina, or Georgia. He was a superman. He was every man.

Contrary to what you might think, historians do not dismiss folklore as mere myth and superstition. People who can't write often pass along history in stories and song. With this in mind, John Henry has been the subject of some pretty serious historical sleuthing.

One trail led Scott Nelson, a professor at the College of William and Mary, to the records of the Virginia State Penitentiary in Richmond. There, he found in the ledger an entry for John William Henry, a young black man from Elizabeth, New Jersey, who had been arrested on charges of larceny in 1866 and sentenced to ten years in jail. At that time, convicts were employed by the thousands to build a railroad line through Virginia to the Ohio River. According to the prison record, John Henry was among them.

Tunneling through the Allegheny Mountains was dangerous—even deadly—work. And it was slow. Collis Huntington, owner of the C&O Railroad, decided to try newfangled steam drills. Much to his disappointment, they kept breaking down on the job. Before he junked them entirely, though, his engineers begged him to give the drills one last chance to prove themselves by testing them against the men who were toiling at the Lewis Tunnel, exactly where John Henry and his work gang had been assigned.

Engineering records from 1870 reveal that, just like the song says, those early drills could not outdrive a man with a hammer in his hand. But was one of those men John Henry? And was there a big showdown? That will have to be left to our imaginations.

Why does the story continue to intrigue us more than a century later? First, it is a tale of courage and sacrifice. Second, and more important, it celebrates all the ordinary men, both black and white, who built the railroads and, by extension, America itself. Some forty thousand died in the construction of the C&O Railroad alone, and many of them were buried in unmarked graves. They may not have headstones, but they do have a song. And they all have one name: John Henry.

Q Who invented the bikini?

A Good question. It's impossible to say for sure, but we do know that in one form or another, the two-piece, bra-and-panty-style garment has been around for a while. Archeologists dug up Minoan drawings from ancient Greece dating back to 1600 BC that depict females donning the scanty fashion, and a large collection of mosaics from Sicily circa AD 400 features athletic ladies posing in little more than their skivvies.

The first women's two-piece garments that exposed the midriff and were designed specifically for swimming appeared in the 1930s. Popularized by movie stars of the time, the top piece often was a bralike halter and the bottom was a wide-legged pair of shorts. These swimsuits were more revealing than their predecessors, but were hardly risqué—they were considerably more modest (no belly buttons bared) than the suits that hit the fashion scene the following decade.

After World War II, two independent French designers made their marks—skimpy ones, at that—on the world of swimwear. Jacques Heim crafted a teeny two-piece that he called the atome, named after the smallest particle known at the time, the atom. He revealed his design on June 14, 1946, and contracted skywriters to fly over the beaches of Cannes to promote it.

The other designer, Louis Reard, realized that he, too, needed a catchy name and a marketing plan for his creation. On July 1, 1946, the United States tested an atomic bomb in the South Pacific, on a tiny atoll named Bikini; whether it was the test or the island, something about the event reputedly sparked Reard's imagination.

Four days later, he introduced his "explosive fashion," the bikini. Skywriters again took to the air, though this time they were hired by Reard. They flew over the French Riviera to promote the bikini as being an even smaller bathing suit than the atome. (Reard was fond of telling people that a two-piece was not a bikini "unless it could be pulled through a wedding ring.")

Unfortunately, Reard could not find a reputable model who would agree to wear his bikini in public, so he settled for a well-known "showgirl." It was a fitting debut for Reard's creation. The bikini sparked immediate outrage: The Vatican declared it immoral, and it was banned in Spain, Portugal, and Italy. But the bikini wouldn't die—today, it is alive and well. Thank goodness.

Q Who decides if a fashion trend is hot?

A Are you asking, "Who's going to claim responsibility for acid-wash jeans, shoulder pads, and parachute pants?"

Those fashions were considered hip not long ago. But crimes of style are meant to be forgiven, right?

We know that fashion is fickle—it's a revolving door of cuts, fabrics, colors, lengths, and embellishments. What's "in" one season might be way "out" the next. (Hello, leg warmers; goodbye, leg warmers.) Just who decides what's hot and what's not? We do.

Big-time designers get the ball rolling by sending waiflike models down runways in Milan who are wearing their latest creations. And trends like ruffles, jewel tones, and slouchy trousers are deemed *au courant* by Anna Wintour and her crew at *Vogue* magazine.

One glimpse of our favorite celebrity walking the red carpet or dancing in a video, and we're style-smitten. Remember the plunging green Versace that Jennifer Lopez wore at the Grammys in 2000? Michael Jackson's red leather jacket in the "Thriller" music video? Of course you do—and maybe you wanted the same look. It's what the American Marketing Association calls the "emulation stage." In the short life cycle of a fashion trend, it's when a look is plastered all over the Internet, television, and women's fashion magazines like *In Style* and *Elle*.

Carrie's wearing a nameplate necklace on *Sex and the City?* Gotta have it. Victoria Beckham's sporting high-waist skinny jeans? Not so much. As consumers, we may not start fashion trends, but we determine which really sizzle through what we choose to buy and wear.

Hey, is that you wearing a Hypercolor T-shirt and fanny pack in that picture? Ouch. But don't worry, they'll be back in style.

Q Why are so many manicurists Vietnamese?

A No, you're not imagining it. In 2008, 43 percent of manicurists in the United States were Vietnamese. The number was even higher in California—80 percent. What's the deal here?

In 1975, as the government of South Vietnam collapsed, refugee camps for Vietnamese immigrants sprang up all over the United States. More than 125,000 people fled the small country that year, hoping to build better lives in America. Their numbers included businessmen and businesswomen, teachers, and government officials. Most left everything they owned behind, and they had to learn the customs and the language of a new country.

Hope Village was a refugee camp near Sacramento, California, that was visited frequently by actress Tippi Hedren. Remember her from *The Birds?* Well, most of the Vietnamese women at the camp didn't, but they were duly impressed by her beautifully manicured nails.

On one visit to the camp, Hedren brought along her manicurist. The refugees, intrigued by this whole manicure deal, saw an opportunity. Over the next few weeks, Hedren's manicurist taught the women how to do nails. Hedren persuaded a beauticians' school in the area to train the refugees, and she even helped them get jobs. Since a professional manicure in those days cost around sixty dollars, most women treated it as a luxury and didn't have their nails done often. The Vietnamese slashed prices in order to bring in more customers—and the discount nail salon was born.

As the women prospered, their friends and family members—even some males—took up the manicure trade. Since 1975, more than one million Vietnamese immigrants have arrived in the United States, and many of their first jobs have been at nail salons. It's a classic American success story—and it's one that continues to unfold.

Q Who was the female Paul Revere?

A Listen, my children, and you shall hear of the midnight ride of ... Sybil Ludington. Sybil who? Almost everyone has heard the story of Paul Revere, who rode from Boston to Lexington on April 18, 1775, to warn his fellow revolutionaries that the British were coming. But how many people know that two years later, on April 26, 1777, sixteen-year-old Sybil Ludington from Fredericksburg—now Kent—New York, mounted her favorite horse, Star, and set off on a similar mission?

Earlier that night, an exhausted messenger had arrived from Danbury, Connecticut, to tell Sybil's father that the town had fallen into British hands. Located about twenty-five miles south of Fredericksburg, Danbury served as a major supply depot for Washington's Continental Army. The Redcoats had not only seized the town, they also had set fire to homes and storehouses. The blaze could be seen for miles.

Henry Ludington, a colonel in the local militia, needed to rally his troops immediately. But whom could he send to alert them? Most of his men were at home on their farms tending to the spring plowing. He could not rouse them himself; he had stay put in order to organize the soldiers as they assembled. And the messenger from Danbury was far too tired to travel any farther. What to do?

Henry's eldest daughter, Sybil, volunteered to carry the message, and her father reluctantly consented. Sybil was an accomplished rider, knew how to shoot, and often watched her father drill the militia.

She and her sister Rebecca had guarded the family home while their father was asleep or away. The previous year, she had managed to outsmart a group of Tories who had surrounded the house in the hope of collecting a large bounty offered by the British for capturing or killing Sybil's father.

Using muskets, a bunch of lit candles, and the support of her seven younger siblings, Sybil fooled the group of loyalists into believing that the house was well-protected by armed militia. Now, Sybil was ready to do her patriotic duty again.

Astride Star, she galloped over rain-sodden trails, through dark and dense forest, and over pitted, rock-studded roads during a thunderstorm. The terrain was dangerous in more ways than one: A young woman traveling alone was vulnerable to attack and other violence.

"Muster at Ludington's!" she cried, stopping at the farmhouses of the men in her father's regiment. By dawn, Sybil had traveled more than forty miles, and most of the four hundred American soldiers under Sybil's father's command were ready to march against the British forces.

Sybil's bravery has not been forgotten. She was commemorated with a bicentennial stamp by the U.S. Post Office in 1976, the state of New York erected a monument to mark her route, and she is the subject of several children's books. There is even a poem about Sybil, which begins:

> Listen, my children, and you shall hear
> Of a lovely feminine Paul Revere
> Who rode an equally famous ride
> Through a different part of the countryside,
> Where Sybil Ludington's name recalls
> A ride as daring as that of Paul's.

Chapter Three

WEIRD SCIENCE AND TECHNOLOGY

Q Is dropped toast more likely to land buttered side down?

A No need to break out the lab coat, bread loaf, toaster, and butter stick—we'll save you the time and expense. Yes, buttered toast is more likely to hit the floor buttered side down, at least in normal breakfast table mishaps.

In 1995, a scientist named Robert Matthews published calculations that predicted this to be true. In 2000, he proved it with the help of a thousand British school children. In nearly ten thousand trials, he found that the toast landed buttered side down 62 percent of the time.

Does this mean that the universe is out to get us? Maybe. But there's a less malevolent explanation. Imagine what happens when you accidentally drop a piece of toast. There's a good chance that after it slides off your plate or out of your fingers, it will turn end over end. It keeps rotating as it falls, but unless you're eating breakfast on the rim of the Grand Canyon, it won't have very far to go before it hits the ground. There's usually only enough time for the toast to make about half a rotation before it lands. Since you have the buttered side up when your toast is on the plate, that side is likely to end up facing down on impact—giving your new carpet a messy taste of that delicious melted butter. Of course, it doesn't always happen this way. Sometimes your toast just falls straight down, and your carpet is saved.

What if you did what comedian Stephen Wright proposed and tied buttered toast to the back of a cat and dropped it? Since cats always land on their feet and toast often lands buttered side down, would the cat and toast simply spin in midair forever? If only. The feline would land on its feet, since cats are especially skilled at the aerial acrobatics that are necessary for safe landings. But then it might roll over and butter your carpet just to spite you.

Q Can you really fry an egg on the sidewalk?

A Claiming that "it's so hot outside that you can fry an egg on the sidewalk!" is an exaggeration—unless you have the proper tools. Eggs must reach 144 to 158 degrees Fahrenheit to change from liquid to solid and be considered cooked, according to the American Egg Board. Even on the most searing summer days, the typical sidewalk falls way short of the 144 degrees necessary to get eggs sizzling and coagulating.

Pavement of any kind is a poor conductor of heat, says Robert Wolke in his book *What Einstein Told His Cook: Kitchen Science Explained.* For starters, when you crack an egg onto pavement, the egg slightly cools the pavement's surface. In order to fry an egg, the temperature of a sidewalk has to climb enough to start and maintain the coagulating process. Lacking a constant flame or source of heat from below or from the sides, pavement can't maintain a temperature that's hot enough to cook eggs evenly. Forget sunny side up—you're likely to end up with a runny mess.

But frying an egg on the sidewalk is not impossible. Just ask the contestants of the Solar Egg Frying Contest, held each Fourth of July in the little town of Oatman, Arizona. People come from far and wide in hope of winning a trophy for "the most edible" solar-cooked egg.

Technically, these people are cheating. Contestants in the Oatman egg fry are allowed the use of mirrors, magnifying glasses, aluminum reflectors, and any kind of homemade cooking surface or contraption they can devise to harness the power of the sun. It also seems that sidewalk cooking is a bit more plausible in Arizona in July: heat is high, humidity is low, and the liquid in the cooking eggs dries out a little faster.

Still, your best bet is to abandon a sidewalk altogether and use a surface similar to that of a frying pan. Spritz a little Pam onto the hood of your '57 Chevy and get cooking. Metal is a much better conductor of heat than concrete.

Q When will jet packs be ready for consumer use?

A Jet packs no longer are just the stuff of James Bond movies—they are a reality. But you need to be rich—part of the jet set, so to speak—to get one.

The jet pack, also known as a rocket belt, has a simplistic aim:

It enables users to avoid clogged streets by taking to the sky. It takes a sophisticated design to accomplish this feat. The device is strapped to the wearer's back and propels him or her off the ground using small rockets.

Much of the jet pack's development is credited to Bell Aerosystems engineer Wendell Moore, who designed the Small Rocket Lift Device in 1953. His shaky, unstable prototype ran on nitrogen gas and generated enough interest to secure a contract from the United States Army. Moore's design evolved to include a 280-pound thrust rocket motor that ran on peroxide, but it only enabled users to stay aloft for only twenty-one seconds. As a result, the Army eventually lost interest. Many subsequent versions were designed, some with wings, but each struggled to address the same challenges, such as flight time, user safety, fuel, and weight.

In 2007, two companies introduced consumer-ready jet packs with lift times approaching nineteen minutes. Colorado-based JetPack International uses standard jet fuel in its model, and

Tecnologia Aeroespacial Mexicana sells a rocket belt that runs on propane. JetPack's model, the T 73, goes for about $200,000, including training.

Both manufacturers have had difficulty finding buyers for their products, which are not user-friendly in addition to carrying hefty price tags. Indeed, jet packs are so trivial that the Federal Aviation Administration has yet to institute licensing regulations for the contraptions.

Q How does a gas pump nozzle know when your tank is full?

A When you've maxed out your credit card, of course. Actually, the system is entirely mechanical and completely impervious to financial matters.

The mechanism at work is a little complicated, but the basic idea is fairly straightforward. As gas flows, it generates suction inside the nozzle, thanks to something called the Venturi effect. A fuel nozzle uses this suction to gauge whether there's any air at the end of the nozzle spout.

In the nozzle, the gas passes through a Venturi ring, a narrow passageway with tiny openings that lead to an air chamber. This air chamber is connected to a long tube that leads to a hole near the end of the nozzle spout, just under the larger hole where the gas comes out. Essentially, this tube is a straw for sucking air from the tank. As the fuel flows through the ring, the suction from the Venturi effect reduces air pressure in the chamber. Air rushes from the tank through the tube to equalize the pressure, in the same way soda rushes through a straw to equalize a drop in pressure in your mouth.

As long as there is room in the tank, the system will keep sucking in air and the pressure in the chamber will stay close to normal atmospheric levels. But when the gasoline reaches the tip of the nozzle, no more air can get through the little hole and the pressure in the chamber drops. This increased suction pulls on a diaphragm connected to the nozzle's shut-off valve, which closes to stop the flow of gasoline.

If you try to keep pumping to "top off" the tank, you might actually be pumping money out of your wallet. According to the Environmental Protection Agency, when there's no room in the tank, extra gas can flow up through vapor recovery lines in the pump that are designed to prevent gas vapor from polluting the atmosphere. As a result, you may be paying to pump gas back into the station's tanks. Haven't you given them enough already?

Q Why does a boomerang come back?

A Because if it didn't, it would just be a stick. Seriously, a boomerang flies in a circle because its simple structure—essentially two wings joined together—combines basic physical forces in a unique way.

We won't beat you over the head with details of wing physics; they could fill a book. The important thing to understand is that a wing diverts the flow of the air rushing past it, which generates lift. In other words, as a wing zips along through air, the air follows the wing's curved shape and leaves the back of the wing moving downward.

This lifts a wing in two ways: The air pushing downward causes an equal and opposite reaction in the wing, which forces the wing upward. At the same time, the moving air creates a disturbance that drives air away from the space above the wing, which creates a drop in air pressure that essentially sucks the wing upward.

The correct way to throw a boomerang—they come in right- and left-handed versions, by the way—is nearly vertically. This allows lift from the two wings to push sideways rather than upward. As the boomerang spins, whichever wing is at top at any particular moment generates more lift than the wing that's at the bottom. Why? Because the top wing is moving through the air more quickly than the bottom one. (Note that if the boomerang were spinning while sitting on a rod, like a helicopter rotor, the same amount of air would be moving past both wings all the time. But because you throw the boomerang, you add forward motion to the mix.)

At the top of the rotation, the wing is spinning forward, in the same direction as the throw. At the bottom of the rotation, the wing is spinning backward, opposite the forward direction of the throw. Since whichever wing is on top is moving forward more quickly (forward motion of the spin plus forward motion of the throw), more air rushes past, which generates more lift.

This extra lift pushes on each wing at the top the spin. However—and this is where things get weird—there's a delayed reaction, and the push doesn't take effect until the wing rotates another ninety degrees. This weird phenomenon of spinning objects is called gyroscopic procession. It's the same thing that makes a bicycle turn when you take your hands off the handles and lean to the left or right: You're pushing on the top of the wheel, but the front of the wheel turns.

As the spinning boomerang flies, lift is constantly pushing sideways on its leading edge. The push gradually turns the boomerang; this makes it travel in a circular path, right back to the thrower. At the end of the flight, the force of the lift has pushed the boomerang on its side, which makes it easier to catch between your hands, like a Frisbee.

Q Who invented the computer mouse?

A Douglas Engelbart. And here's an extra-credit question: When did he do it? Is your guess the 1990s or the 1980s? If so, you're wrong. The correct answer is the 1960s.

Engelbart grew up on a farm, served in the Navy during World War II, and then obtained a PhD. He wound up at the Stanford Research Institute, where he pursued his dream of finding new ways to use computers. Back in the 1950s, computers were room-filling behemoths that fed on punch cards.

Engelbart believed that computers could potentially interact with people and enhance their skills and knowledge; he imagined computer users darting around an ethereal space that was filled with information. Most folks couldn't envision what he had in mind—no one thought of a computer as a personal machine, partially because the models of the day didn't even have keyboards or monitors.

Engelbart set up the Augmentation Research Center lab in 1963 and developed something he called the oNLine System (NLS). Today, we would recognize NLS as word-processing documents with hypertext links, accessed via a graphical user interface and a mouse.

On December 9, 1968, after years of tinkering, Engelbart presented his new technology at the Fall Joint Computer Conference in San Francisco. Engelbart's mouse—with a ball, rollers, and three buttons at the top—was only slightly larger than today's models. It was called a mouse because of its tail (the cord that connected it to the computer), though no one remembers who gave it its name. We do know, however, that engineer Bill English built the first mouse for Engelbart.

To Engelbart's disappointment, his new gadgets—including the mouse—didn't immediately catch on. Some curmudgeons in the audience thought that the ninety-minute demo was a hoax, though it received a standing ovation from most of the computer professionals in attendance. Eventually, Engelbart got the last laugh: His lab hooked up with one at UCLA to launch the ARPANET in October 1969. ARPANET, as any computer geek knows, was a precursor to the Internet.

Engelbart's mouse patent expired in 1987, about the time the device was becoming a standard feature on personal computers. Consequently, he has never received a dime in royalties. But he was never in it for money—Engelbart's motivation was to raise humanity's "Collective IQ," our shared intelligence.

In November 2000, President Clinton presented Engelbart with the National Medal of Technology, the highest honor the nation can award a citizen for technological achievement. Engelbart may not have gotten rich from his computer mouse, but he at least gained a measure of lasting fame.

Q What's the process for shrinking a head?

A Well into the twentieth century, the Amazonian Jivaro tribe made a point of returning from battle toting the shrunken heads of its enemies. Talk about unique souvenirs.

These heads, or *tsantsa,* were a central element of the Jivaro practice of blood revenge. If someone from a neighboring tribe—or even a different group within the Jivaro tribe—wronged your family, it was essential that you exact revenge on his kin. The result was a cycle of murder, head collection, and hurt feelings.

Not only was *tsantsa* the best revenge, but it was also the best way to prevent supernatural harassment from your victim. The Jivaro believed that shrinking the victim's head captured his soul, keeping him from moving on to the afterlife, where he could torment you and your dead ancestors.

As you might expect, the recipe for a tiny head is a tad gruesome. The avengers decapitated the offending party—or one of his relatives—and looped a band through the head's mouth and neck hole, making a sort of handle. Then they high-tailed it to a secluded camp by a river, where they sliced open the back of the head, carefully peeled away the skin, and tossed the skull into the river as an offering to a spirit they believed lived in the anaconda snake.

Next, they sewed the eyes shut, fastened the mouth closed with wooden skewers, and placed the head in boiling water for up to two hours. The boiling process shrank the head to about a third of its normal size. After boiling, the Jivaro began the trip back home, continuing to work on the *tsantsa* along the way.

They turned the skin inside out and scraped away any remaining flesh before turning it right-side out and sewing up the back of the head. The Jivaron then put scorching rocks inside the head and filled and refilled it with hot sand, drying the skin and shrinking it further. Next, they removed the skewers from the lips and tied them shut with long lengths of string.

The head then was hung over a fire for hardening and blackening and was covered in charcoal to seal in the spirit of the dead individual. Finally, the Jivaro cut a hole in the top of the head and inserted a stick with a loop of sturdy string tied to it. And there it was: a perfect shrunken head to wear around the neck.

Back home, the *tsantsa* were the centerpieces of several feasts. The shrinking process and the feasts were essential requirements for exacting revenge. After that purpose was served, however, the heads no longer were important and often ended up as toys for kids. The tribe even set up a profitable side business, trading the heads to foreigners for guns and other goods, but the Peruvian and Ecuadorian governments cracked down on the practice in the 1930s and 1940s. Party poopers.

Q Why is some clothing marked "dry clean only"?

A That little label inside your shirt is officially called a Permanent Care Label (PCL), and it's required by the United States government's consumer protection agency, otherwise known as the Federal Trade Commission (FTC). According to FTC rules, manufacturers and importers must attach these itchy little labels to all textile products. While they may serve to irritate the heck out of the back of your neck, PCLs are intended to help you make informed choices and properly care for your purchased apparel.

Do you want to wear that super-soft cashmere cowl neck you bought at Bendel's (not on sale) more than once? Then you had best pay attention to its PCL. The FTC's Permanent Care Labeling Rule mandates that the tag must recommend at least one safe laundering method. So when a garment is marked "dry clean only," the manufacturer is warning you that this particular piece can't be washed safely at home-not in the washing machine and not by hand.

Why not? Some textiles will be irreparably harmed if washed in water. They will shrink, fade, wrinkle, stretch out of shape, or lose delicate details like beading, ruching, or lace. Wool is notorious for shrinking in the wash; acetate, velvet, suede, leather, and fur won't fare too well in the Maytag, either.

But how's this for a spin? Many garments that are labeled "dry clean only" might in fact be washable. Despite the FTC rule that manufacturers and importers "possess specific, reliable evidence that that garment will be harmed by washing," some companies slap the "dry clean only" label on clothes whether they have that evidence or not.

What does that mean for you? You might be able to save a few bucks by carefully laundering some of your "dry clean only" clothing at home. This isn't a risk you should take with anything for which you paid a lot of money, or anything you really love and wish to keep (i.e., your wedding dress or your husband's Burberry suit). But certain "dry clean only" fabrics—including rayon, linen, and silk—might just survive a gentle cold-water wash with mild detergent.

Willing to take a gamble with your "dry clean only" garments? Fine, but don't be too miffed if you have to pass that shrunken chiffon blouse down to your thinner sister.

Q Is it better to leave your computer on or off at night?

A Ah, one of the great nerd debates of all time. It's turned brother against brother and divided IT departments everywhere.

At the risk of enraging one geek camp, we're going to side with the turn-it-off crew. When you shut down your computer and start it up again, the operating system clears data that has collected in the computer's memory all day, runs through various system checks, and generally cleans house. In the same way that restarting your computer can sometimes clear up big problems, shutting it down and starting it up periodically can make the software run better.

You may also prolong your computer's life by giving the fan a break now and then. Most modern computers go into a sleep mode when they're idle, which means many of the components aren't doing much. But the fan keeps going, wearing down its various moving pieces. Meanwhile, it's also sucking more dust and other debris into the computer.

And while it's not going to help you retire early, shutting down will save you money. Turning your computer and monitor off every night could save you fifty to one hundred dollars a year or more, depending upon the cost of electricity in your area.

The main argument for leaving your computer on is that powering up and shutting down puts extra strain on your hard drive and other hardware components, which makes them wear out more quickly. This was probably true back in the old days (the 1990s and earlier), but it's doubtful today. Modern computers are a lot heartier, and there's no clear evidence that switching on and off leads to hardware failures. Something else will probably fry your computer long before this type of wear and tear does.

A secondary argument is that it's better to leave your computer on so that it can regulate its own temperature, running the fan if the hardware gets too hot but never dipping into dangerously cold territory either. Again, there's not much evidence to back up this notion. Unless you're keeping your computer on the beach or at an Antarctic research station, it probably isn't going to encounter the types of temperature swings that cause damage.

Some nerds will tell you that booting up uses a lot of electricity, so it's more economical to leave your computer on. This definitely isn't true. While booting up takes a bit more energy than normal operation, it doesn't come close to the amount of electricity you save by leaving the computer off for even an hour.

All that being said, leaving your computer on constantly doesn't really shorten your computer's life, and turning it off at night doesn't amount to significant savings. If you can't stand waiting a couple minutes to get to the Internet, leave it on. The world—or the computer—won't come to an end.

Q Why does the sun make hair lighter but skin darker?

A The key here is a substance called melanin—a bunch of chemicals that combine as a pigment for your skin and hair. In addition to dictating hair and skin colors, melanin protects people from the harmful effects of ultraviolet (UV) light. It does this by converting the energy from UV light to heat, which is relatively harmless. Melanin converts more than 99 percent of this energy, which leaves only a trace amount to mess with your body and cause gnarly problems like skin cancer.

When you head out for a day in the sun and don't put on sunscreen, the sun delivers a massive blast of heat and UV light directly to your skin and hair. The skin reacts to this onslaught by ramping up the production of melanin in order to combat that nasty UV radiation. This is where things get a bit tricky. There are two types of melanin: pheomelanin (which is found in greater abundance in people with lighter skin and hair) and eumelanin (which is found in greater abundance in people with darker skin and hair).

If you're unlucky—that is, if your skin has a lot of pheomelanin—the sun can damage the skin cells, causing a splotchy, reddish sunburn and maybe something worse down the road. After the sunburn, the skin peels to rid itself of all these useless, damaged cells. And then you get blisters and oozing pus, and your skin explodes—no, it ain't pretty. People whose skin has an increased production of eumelanin, on the other hand, are saved from these side effects—the sun simply gives their skin a smooth, dark sheen.

And what's the impact on hair? Well, hair is dead—it's just a clump of protein. By the time hair pokes through the scalp, it doesn't contain any melanin-producing cells. So when the sun damages it by destroying whatever melanin is in it, your mane is pretty much toast—no new melanin can be produced. Consequently, your hair loses its pigment until new, darker strands grow.

The moral of the story? Be sensible in the sun—it's a massive flaming ball of gas, and it doesn't care about your health.

Chapter Four

FOOD AND DRINK

Q Are organic foods better for you?

A It all depends on what you mean by "better." If you are talking about better nutrition, there's no conclusive evidence that shows that organic food is more nutritious than conventionally grown food. Sure, there are a few studies that say that organic produce contains higher levels of vitamin C, minerals, and antioxidants, but these higher levels are negligible; they're not likely to improve your overall health.

So why are people loading up their grocery carts with everything from organic apples to organic strip steak? The real benefit of going organic is safety. "If you're talking about pesticides, the evidence is pretty conclusive," says John Reganold, a professor of soil science at Washington State University. "Your chances of getting pesticide residues are much less with organic food." A large-scale study by the Consumers Union found that organically grown crops have about a third of the pesticide residue of conventionally grown produce.

Why is this important? Laboratory studies have linked pesticides to health problems, including birth defects, nerve damage, and cancer. Some pesticides pose risks to the development of infants and children, hindering their bodies' ability to absorb nutrients that are necessary for normal growth. However, most experts agree that the low levels of pesticides that are found in or on conventionally grown fruits and vegetables pose only a small health risk; they're well below what the Environmental Protection Agency (EPA) has deemed unsafe.

The real question is whether low levels of pesticide exposure can add up to increased health risks over time. No one can say for sure—do you want to be the EPA's guinea pig? That's one factor to consider when deciding whether to buy organic foods. For most shoppers, though, the decision comes down to what they can afford: On average, organic foods—especially meat and milk—can cost anywhere from 50 to 100 percent more than conventional goods.

The good news is that if you want to reduce your exposure to the pesticides in food, you don't have to buy organic across the board. According to *Consumer Reports,* the best strategy is to buy organic versions of foods whose conventional counterparts carry the highest levels of pesticide residues and potential toxins. These include apples, baby food, bell peppers, celery, cherries, dairy products, eggs, imported grapes, meat, nectarines, peaches, pears, potatoes, poultry, red raspberries, spinach, and strawberries.

Ready to hit the market? Just remember to read food labels carefully. The word "organic" on the label doesn't necessarily signify a healthier option. In fact, many organic foods are as high in sugar, salt, fat, and calories as their conventionally produced counterparts. There is such a thing as organic chocolate ice cream, you know.

Q Will coffee stunt your growth?

A This is one of the many white lies that your mother told you. Don't be mad at her, though—she was only thinking of your health. And in an indirect way, she was right. Nutritionists recommend that growing children keep away from super-caffeinated drinks, coffee included. But it's not because these concoctions affect a child's height—research shows coffee has zero impact on growth.

At one time, coffee was believed to cause osteoporosis, a disease that decreases bone density and can result in fractures and breaks. Fractures of the spine can have horrible consequences, including back pain, deformity, and loss of height. Hence, your mother's concern that coffee would stunt your growth.

But the connection between caffeine and osteoporosis was ultimately debunked. Bone expert Robert P. Heaney concluded from his studies that research linking coffee and osteoporosis had been focused on the elderly, many of whom had replaced milk and other calcium-rich drinks with coffee. In doing so, these people were cutting out a source of nutrition and doing nothing to compensate for the subsequent lack of calcium.

Just one glass of milk per day can make up for this calcium deficiency, according to a 1988–1991 study of 980 women in Rancho Bernardo, California. The women, ages fifty to ninety-eight, underwent bone-density tests for the duration of the study. Part of the study included a self-reported list of foods and drinks that each woman consumed in a day. The results showed that bone density was indeed decreased in women who drank at least two cups of coffee each day; however, such a change was not seen in women who offset their coffee intake by drinking at least one glass of milk per day.

But back to kids. They can drink coffee without worrying about stunting their growth, but there might be other problems involved. High doses of caffeine throughout the day can lead to anxiety and jitteriness, and can also affect sleep patterns. For kids, especially those who have a hard time sitting still in the first place, too much caffeine can make it difficult to concentrate in school.

Moderation is the key. A soda or a cup of coffee here and there won't hurt you. It might make you irritable and shaky, but it won't make you short.

Q Why do we drink eggnog at Christmas?

A Nothing says Christmas quite like the mixture of raw eggs, hard liquor, and fragrant spice that we call eggnog. What could be more festive than this dubiously textured, high-alcohol punch? Sure, there are plenty of ways to get plastered during the holiday season, but only eggnog can incline the drinker toward that unholy trinity of drunkenness, salmonella poisoning, and heart disease.

But it's not just about getting wasted. You can buy non-alcoholic eggnog—heavily processed and artificially flavored—at any grocery store. It might be because the holiday season has traditionally been a time of rich foods and sweet desserts—and isn't a glass of eggnog basically a Christmas cookie in liquid form?

This supermarket concoction is the most modern example of a venerable (and patriotic) tradition. Eggnog dates back to colonial America. George Washington is said to have been so fond of the drink that he developed his own recipe, which included whiskey, rum, brandy, and sherry. (That'll warm your Valley Forge!)

George wasn't the only Virginia farmer-politician who enjoyed the tipple. Another story has it that in the early days of the Virginia House of Delegates, which now is the oldest legislature in the western hemisphere, a Christmas-season session had to be adjourned because the members were so loaded on eggnog that they were in a "helpless condition."

There are some Scrooges who claim that eggnog isn't really an American innovation at all. And it's true that our founding fathers weren't the first to mix eggs and booze to make a delicious drink. There are earlier English punches that combine egg yolks with wine or beer—one explanation of the origin of the word "egg-nog" claims that "nog" is a reference to a specific type of English beer. And some reckless speculators have guessed that our beloved beverage was inspired by a French recipe. *Mon Dieu!*

In all fairness, let's give credit where credit is due. Even if we didn't think up the idea, we gave it a catchy name, made it stronger, and drank the hell out of it. And after all, isn't that what Christmas is all about?

Q Did the French really invent French toast?

A Not so fast, *mon ami*. There are plenty of conflicting stories about which country was the first to dunk day-old bread into milk and fry it.

The accounts go all the way back to ancient Rome.

Take a look at *Apicius de re Coquinaria*—a collection of Roman cookery recipes that was compiled in the fourth or fifth century AD and translated to English in 1936 by professional chef Joseph Dommers Vehling—and you will find a dish titled *Aliter Dulcia* ("Another Sweet"). The recipe for *Aliter Dulcia* goes as follows: "Break [slice] fine white bread, crust removed, into rather large pieces which soak in milk [and beaten eggs]. Fry in oil, cover with honey, and serve."

Sounds similar to the golden-brown slices topped with maple syrup that you find at IHOP today, right? Still, no one can be sure that the *Apicius* recipe represents the first French toast. But it is clear that similar bread dishes were popular throughout Medieval Europe, albeit with varying names. In Germany, the recipe was called *arme ritter;* in England, *suppe dorate;* and in Portugal, *fatias douradas,* which literally translates to "golden slices of bread."

Interestingly enough, if you go to France, you won't find French toast, or even *Toast à la Française,* on the menu. Their version of eggy bread is called *pain perdu* ("lost bread"), a likely reference to the reclamation of stale bread that would otherwise be lost to the garbage or the pigeons. In the United States, French-speaking cooks in Cajun areas of Louisiana make *pain perdu* using thick slices of local French bread and a topping of cinnamon, powdered sugar, and Louisiana cane syrup.

The French might lay claim to bringing the French toast recipe to the United States, but some people offer up an entirely different explanation for the name. According to this alternate theory, French toast is an all-American creation, first made by Joseph French at his roadside tavern in Albany, New York, circa 1724. Though Mr. French wished to credit himself for the sweet, golden breakfast treat he supposedly invented, he listed it on the menu as French toast—not French's toast. Why? Because he didn't know how to use an apostrophe.

So does French toast have its roots in ancient culinary history or an unfortunate grammatical oversight? When you have a plate that's piled high with pan-fried toast, powdered sugar, strawberries, and syrup, who really cares?

Q Why does fruitcake keep so long?

A That's easy: It's loaded with booze. No mold can grow in that much alcohol. Fruitcakes start with fruit—fresh or dried—that is typically soaked for a week in port wine, bourbon, or dark rum. When the cake batter is mixed, a cup of whisky, brandy, or another equally potent liquor is likely to be one of the ingredients.

Alcohol is sometimes added even after the cake is baked. Some recipes call for the fruitcake to be sprinkled with brandy once a week for a month or more. If you don't want to go the sprinkling route, you can soak a towel in brandy and wrap it around the cake. A few old-fashioned cooks bake the cake with a cup placed in the middle in order to create a deep depression. When the cake cools, the depression is filled with brandy or rum, which soaks into the cake. This process can be repeated again and again as the cake absorbs each dose of alcohol.

Not every cook wants to get the family drunk on fruitcake. Some recipes leave the booze out and substitute fruit juice. These tee-totaler cakes can last a long time if they are stored in airtight tins, but alcohol is the key ingredient of a true fruitcake.

Early versions of fruitcake were carried on long campaigns by Roman legions and the Crusaders. Sometimes, fruitcake that was made from a past year's harvest was shared to invoke blessings on the current year's harvest.

Delayed consumption is a fruitcake tradition. A fruitcake that is given as a gift is rarely eaten right away. Indeed, "regifting" is a fruitcake ritual, and some of the most legendary fruitcake creations last for decades.

Q What exactly is a carb?

A Poor carbohydrates. These organic compounds were happily minding their own business and fueling every human body on the planet until diet gurus, including Dr. Robert Atkins, came along and gave them a bad name. Carbs are the primary energy source for our muscles and brains, so it's time to cut them some slack.

When we mention carbs, we're talking about a lot more than white bread and potatoes. As a broad category, carbohydrates include sugars, starches, and fiber. They can be found in a lot of foods (albeit in varying quantities), including grains, fruits and vegetables, and dairy products.

There are two classes of carbohydrates that you should get to know: simple and complex. Both are made up of units of sugar, but they differ in size, number of sugar molecules, and ease of bodily absorption.

Simple carbohydrates are found in fruits and vegetables in the forms of glucose and fructose, beet or cane sugar in the form of sucrose, and milk in the form of lactose. Simple carbs can comprise a single sugar or two single sugars that are linked together. For example, sucrose (common table sugar) is made from single-sugar glucose linked to single-sugar fructose.

Complex carbohydrates are starches and fibers that are commonly found in whole grains, starchy vegetables, and legumes (a fancy name for beans). As their name indicates, complex carbs are indeed more complicated than their simple counterparts. They're made of multiple glucose sugar molecules that are linked together in long, branching chains called polymers.

Simple carbohydrates are absorbed into the body very quickly—that's why a candy bar gives you a "sugar rush." Complex carbohydrates are absorbed more slowly. Digestive enzymes in the small intestine need time to break the long chains of glucose into smaller links and eventually into single molecules. Once that's done, the glucose molecules are absorbed into the bloodstream. This makes your blood glucose levels rise, and the pancreas gets the hint to start secreting insulin. The insulin helps to move the sugar out of your blood and into your muscles and brain for energy.

Needless to say, carbs aren't necessarily bad. Ever hear about runners "carb-loading" the night before a long-distance race? Go and enjoy a plate of spaghetti!

Q What was the most costly meal ever?

A The most costly meal ever was consumed in the summer of 2001 at the swanky London restaurant Pétrus. A six-man party laid out £44,000 ($62,700) for the experience, and five from the group also paid with their jobs.

The big spenders were Barclays Capital bankers who were celebrating the closure of a deal. Pétrus is known for its high-priced wines, many of which it bottles, and the six diners sent corks a-flying. They drank 1945, 1946, and 1947 Bordeaux wines, as well as a 1900 Chateau d'Yquem dessert wine.

A typical three-course meal at Pétrus cost about £50 (about $100) at the time of the bankers' visit. It's unclear what the bankers ordered, but it doesn't really matter—a February 2002 article in the New York Times states that the restaurant was so impressed by the wine selections of the bankers that the food cost was stricken from the bill. The bankers were left to pony up for the wine (which came to more than $60,000) and a few other items, including beer.

The diners initially paid for their Pétrus experience with their own money, but they later submitted the cost on their expense accounts. Five of the bankers were fired. (The sixth had just begun working at the bank and may have been shown mercy because he didn't know any better and because he immediately informed his superiors about the meal.)

At the time, Barclays was restructuring and laying off workers. The Times article says that the bank "was trying to project a new sobriety as an anecdote to the excesses of the 1990s," so it probably did not appreciate the publicity—Pétrus even kept the bill as a memento.

If the human cost isn't taken into account, the most expensive meal ever was consumed at the Dome Restaurant in Bangkok by a group of fifteen diners in February 2007. The bill was 15 million Thai baht, which comes out to $450,000, or $30,000 per diner. The meal stretched over ten courses, beginning with foie gras crème brulee and concluding hours later with a gingerbread pyramid with caramel ice cream. As with the bankers at Pétrus, wine is what made the bill so hefty. The difference is, the Dome Restaurant diners weren't soon looking for new jobs.

Q Why do fruits and vegetables change colors as they ripen?

A Brilliant color is one way to tell if your bananas, apples, tomatoes, and berries are sweet, juicy, and ready to eat. Ever bite into a green banana? That's bitter, brother!

How and why do fruits and vegetables change color? Well, you know how every autumn the leaves turn from green to rich shades of yellow, red, and brown? Aging—or ripening—fruits and vegetables go through a similar process.

Most unripe fruits and veggies are hard, sour, and—you guessed it—green. That green color is largely due to the presence of chlorophyll. (Quick flashback to science class: That's the green pigment found in all green plants. It's vital for photosynthesis, which allows plants to get energy from sunlight.) As growing fruits and vegetables mature, rising levels of acid and enzymes cause the green chlorophyll pigments to break down. That's when your produce begins to show its true hues.

Bananas and certain varieties of apples have vivid skins of yellow and red, respectively, waiting to emerge from underneath that green layer of chlorophyll. Other fruits, like tomatoes, make brand-new color compounds (in their case, glossy red-orange ones) as their chlorophyll begins to wane.

As for peppers, their final coloration depends on their degree of ripeness. No, those aren't different varieties of bell peppers at the grocery store—it just so happens that peppers are vegetables that are good to eat at any stage. They change from green (unripe) to yellow and orange (semi-ripe) to red (fully ripe). That's why green peppers are slightly bitter, while the red ones taste sweet.

What does this all have to do with the autumn leaves? The changing colors of falling leaves and ripening fruits and vegetables is simply a sign of plant senescence (a fancy term biologists use to describe the natural process of deterioration with age). The brilliant tints that are found on ripe fruit and vegetable peels are comprised of active and healthy antioxidants. Eat some every day—preferably before they turn brown and mushy.

Q What's the difference between brandy and cognac?

A Cognac is to brandy what champagne is to sparkling wine. Does that help? If not, try this: More than anything, the distinction between cognac and brandy is geographical.

Cognac is a type of brandy that is made exclusively from the grapes that grow in a specific region of France. Connoisseurs say that cognac is perhaps the finest of all brandies. The clerk at the corner liquor store, meanwhile, is more concerned about the fact that it's the most expensive brandy you can buy; it's behind the counter, so please ask nicely.

Brandy is no more nor less than distilled, fermented fruit juice. Anything that's simply called "brandy" is made from fermented grapes, like wine. When brandy is made from other fruits, it's indicated in the name. An example is apple brandy, which is produced from cider.

As one of the earliest forms of distilled wine, brandy has a distinguished place in the history of spirits. Distilled wine was the original hard liquor, and it was popularized by the court physicians of Renaissance-era Europe (who thought it had medicinal properties). They got the idea of distillation—which purifies the drink and increases its alcohol content—from Arab alchemists. The word "brandy" itself derives from the Dutch *brandewijn* ("burnt wine"). It has been widely enjoyed for more than five hundred years, and it really was carried around by Saint Bernard dogs in tiny kegs in the Swiss Alps.

But you don't need to be snowbound to enjoy its warming properties. So in the words of the poet Busta Rhymes, "Pass the Courvoisier."

Q Why does yeast make dough rise?

A Croissant. Brioche. San Francisco sourdough. If not for the modest, single-celled fungus known as yeast, we would be condemned to a life of lavash (a.k.a. flat, airless cracker bread).

Yeast can turn a glob of dough into a beautifully risen baguette, and the process is really quite simple. Yeast is a living microscopic organism that doesn't require much to work its magic—just moisture (water), food (sugar or starch), and a warm (seventy to eighty-five degrees Fahrenheit), nurturing environment. When mixed with water and flour to make bread, yeast is truly in a happy place. It feeds on the starchy nutrients that are found in the flour and, through the process of fermentation, converts these nutrients into ethanol and carbon dioxide gas.

This carbon dioxide moves into air bubbles within the bread dough. If the dough is a strong, elastic ball of gluten mesh (like it ought to be), the gas will get trapped within these air bubbles and inflate them. As more and more of these tiny air bubbles fill up, the dough begins to rise and expand.

Once the bread is in the oven, heat kills the yeast and burns off the alcohol. And while yeast is mostly known as a leavening agent, it also contributes to bread's flavor.

Q What does humble pie taste like?

A Which would you rather swallow: your pride or a mouthful of deer gizzard? Original recipes for humble pie included the heart, liver, and other internal organs of a deer, cow, or boar. Talk about your awful offal!

The term "humble pie" derives from "umble pie," which dates back roughly to fourteenth-century England. The term "numbles," then later "umbles," referred to those aforementioned, um, *select* bits of a deer carcass. Umble pie was eaten by servants, whose lords feasted on the more palatable cuts of venison or whatever beast was being served. If meat was on the menu and you were eating umble pie, you were likely in a lower or more inferior position in society. The transition from the original term to the pun "humble pie" was an easy one, given that some English dialects silence the "h" at the beginning of a word.

For some unfathomable reason, modern recipes for humble pie do exist, although these call, mercifully, for cuts of beef or other meat. Others are more customary dessert pies with sweet fillings that inspire humility only when you're in the presence of a bathroom scale.

The next time you've done someone wrong, just apologize, take your lumps, wait for time to heal the wound, and consider yourself fortunate. It's better to spend "thirty days in the hole," to quote the 1970s British supergroup Humble Pie, than to eat boar's intestines.

Chapter Five

ANIMAL KINGDOM

Q Which is the world's most poisonous creature?

A There is no way to answer this question scientifically. To do so, in the words of Otter from *Animal House,* "would take years and cost thousands of lives." Mouse lives, at least; you would have to be willing to sacrifice a few million rodents to test the toxins from the known deadly animals and then extrapolate from those findings to humans.

But we can speculate on such a joyously gruesome topic. Many have suggested that the winner would be *Chironex fleckeri,* one of several types of box jellyfish, which technically aren't even jellyfish. (They are cubozoans; jellyfish are scyphozoans.) This

Australian marine stinger is particularly deadly; its venom can kill sixty humans in three minutes. Not only are these bad boys lethal, having accounted for up to one hundred human deaths in the past century—they're also freaky. As Dan Nilsson of the University of Lund in Sweden puts it, "These are fantastic creatures with twenty-four eyes, four parallel brains, and sixty arseholes."

Let's talk about other potential candidates, if only to satisfy our curiosity. *Discovery Magazine* suggests that the poison arrow frog and certain salamanders as contenders for the most-poisonous title. "Just two micrograms of toxin from the poison arrow frog is enough to kill a human," the magazine states, then notes for emphasis that the ink in the period of a sentence is three times that volume.

Discovery Magazine also says that the ugly stonefish—probably the world's most venomous fish—and the inland taipan snake of Australia should be given consideration. But tree-huggers could note, with some objective evidence, that the most poisonous animal is man. Dioxins, among many other deadly poisons, didn't exist until we invented them.

Q Can an octopus open a jar?

A The evidence is in a video on YouTube.com. As Strauss's "Thus Spake Zarathustra" (a.k.a. the theme from *2001: A Space Odyssey*) swells in the background, Violet the octopus unfurls a snaky tentacle and grasps a closed jar that contains a crab. Then, much like a skilled magician draping a handkerchief over a top hat, it covers the jar with its body. A few minutes later, the jar reemerges...without the lid. Or the crab.

Violet isn't the only octopus that can perform this nifty trick. Octi, a resident of New Zealand's National Aquarium, regularly entertains visitors with its ability to extract food from a variety of sealed jars. According to the aquarium's staff, Octi is a friendly, gentle creature that enjoys playing with toys and often reaches out to touch the hands of its keepers—at least when there are no jars around to work on.

So how does an octopus unscrew a lid? Suction. The underside of an octopus's arms and body are cov-ered with highly sensitive suction cups that each contain up to ten thousand neurons. These cups convey a wealth of information to the brain, allowing the octo-pus to vary pressure on the lid and eventually twist it off.

In the wild, an octopus can pry open the most stubborn clam. But since potential meals don't come packed in jars at the bottom of the ocean, the question naturally arises: How does an octopus learn that these strange glass cylinders in the zoo are a source of snacks? The answer: It uses its natural curiosity and plenty of smarts.

Though they may not look very bright, octopuses, also known as cephalopods, are among the intellectual giants of the deep. They have the largest brains of all invertebrates relative to body weight. Their brains are divided into lobes and resemble those of birds or mammals more closely than they do those of fish. Jennifer Mather, a psychologist at Canada's University of Lethbridge, has conducted studies that suggest that octopuses can even be right-eyed or left-eyed, much like humans, who are neurologically wired to favor the right or left hand.

Mather is a pioneer in the field of octopus intelligence. She believes that octopuses have distinct personalities and are adept at some relatively complex tasks. What's more, biologist Jean Boal of Millersville University in Pennsylvania has tested their navigational skills with underwater mazes and has given them high marks for geographical memory.

And when it comes to camouflage, they're champs, according to cephalopod expert Roger Hanlon. At the Woods Hole Marine Biological Laboratory in Massachusetts, he has observed an octopus quickly change shape and color, transforming itself into an innocent-looking rock drifting along the ocean floor.

What's the I.Q. of an average octopus? This is a mystery scientists are still trying to solve. In the meantime, we at least know that one of these creatures can help you open a stubborn pickle jar.

Q Why do gnats travel in swarms?

A Imagine it's a junior-high dance. The girls are gyrating on the dance floor; the guys are huddled in a testosterone-filled mass along the edge of the room, waiting to be asked to dance. This is a somewhat accurate parallel to gnat behavior.

When you see a swarm of gnats, it is most likely made up entirely of males. Where are the ladies? They're off singing, dancing, or sucking blood—you know, the frivolous stuff.

The purpose of the big swarm is for the males to make themselves as visible as possible to the females. Each of these young males is waiting to be chosen as a mate. Often, the gnats will form the swarm in a shaft of light in order to make their presence even more obvious. Noticing all of this commotion, the female will buzz into the wall of manhood and pick out a lucky gnat.

Not every male will mate—gnats live for just a few weeks, so they don't have a lot of opportunities to get lucky. Besides, the swarm doesn't serve the interests of the individual; its function is to ensure the survival of the species. In their short time on this earth, these bugs have to reproduce. Otherwise, it's bye-bye, gnats.

Q How come hibernating animals don't starve?

A They binge, then go comatose. Does this sound like something that's happened to you after you polished off a quart of Häagen-Dazs? Can you imagine that food coma lasting all winter?

Animals that hibernate have triggers that warn them to glut themselves for the winter ahead. As the days get shorter and colder, the critters' internal clocks—which mark time through fluctuations of hormones, neurotransmitters, and amino acids—tell them to fill up and shut down. Bingeing is important; if these creatures don't build up enough fat, they won't survive. The fat that they store for hibernation is brown (rather than white, like human body fat) and collects near the brain, heart, and lungs.

Animals have a number of reasons for hibernating. Cold-blooded creatures such as snakes and turtles adjust their body temperatures according to the weather; in winter, their blood runs so cold that many of their bodily functions essentially stop. Warm-blooded rodents can more easily survive the extreme chills of winter, but they have a different problem: finding food. They most likely developed their ability to hibernate as a way of surviving winter's dearth of munchies.

After an animal has heeded the biological call to pig out, its metabolism starts to slow down. As it hibernates, some bodily functions—digestion, the immune system—shut down altogether. Its heartbeat slows to ten or fewer beats per minute, and its senses stop registering sounds and smells. The animal's body consumes much less fuel than normal—its metabolism can be as low as 1 percent of its normal rate. The stored fat, then, is enough to satisfy the minimal demands of the animal's body, provided the creature found enough to eat in the fall and is otherwise healthy.

It can take hours or even days for the animal's body temperature to rise back to normal after it awakens from hibernation. But time is of the essence—the beast desperately needs water, and thirst drives it out of its nest. However, the animal is groggy and slow of foot—it walks like a drunk—so it can be easy prey if it doesn't hydrate quickly.

Which animals hibernate? Small ones, mostly—cold-blooded and warm-blooded critters alike. The first category includes snakes, lizards, frogs, and tortoises; the second includes dormice, hedgehogs, skunks, and bats.

But what about the bear, the animal that is most closely associated with hibernation? Here's a shocker: Bears don't hibernate. They slow down, sleep a lot, and lose weight during winter, but they don't truly hibernate. So if you're ever taking a peaceful nature walk on a sunny winter morn, beware. A bear might be out there.

Q Are cats the only animals that bury their waste?

A Technically, cats aren't the only animals that bury their waste. We humans have been burying our bodily waste for thousands of years, and all signs point toward the continuance of this habit. Civilizations would be overrun by stink if we didn't.

But in terms of "lower" animals, cats are indeed the only animals that have the courtesy to dispose of their droppings. The only other animal that possesses an inclination to do something special with its feces is the chimpanzee, an animal that will sometimes chuck turds at rival chimps in fits of anger. Every other animal just lets the turds fall where they will.

The house cat's habit of covering its feces probably goes back to its ancestors in the wild. In nature, cats sometimes bury their waste in an effort to hide it from predators and rival cats. In effect, it's the opposite of using urine to mark territory; in an effort to remain incognito, cats do their best to hide any trace of their presence.

By the same token, a dominant cat will leave its poop anywhere it pleases within its territory in order to scare off trespassing felines. A pile of fly-covered waste, and the distinctive smell that wafts from that pile, functions like a BEWARE OF CAT sign. For another cat to ignore this warning would be to invite trouble in the form of teeth and claws.

Your house cat's tendency to bury its feces in a litter box may be a sign that it recognizes your dominance in the house. And if it uses the litter box but neglects to cover its leavings—as some cats do—it may be your tabby's way of acknowledging a kind of shared dominance over the abode.

You needn't worry about your place in the pecking order until you come home and find urine stains in the corners of the room and feces in the middle of the floor. At that point, you are trespassing on your cat's territory—sitting on *its* couch, watching *its* television, popping *its* popcorn—and you'd better start paying rent...or prepare to face the terrible wrath of the tabby cat.

Q Why doesn't a spider get caught in its own web?

A "Oh, what a tangled web we weave," Sir Walter Scott opined. Scott was referring to the complications that arise from deception. Tell a lie and you're bound to cover it up with another. Eventually, you forget which lie you told to whom, and then, well, you're screwed. (Not that we know anything about that.) Even though Scott probably knew next to nothing about arachnids, he was surprisingly accurate with his analogy.

A spiderweb seems to cling to just about everything: flies, gnats, mosquitoes, even other spiders. And just about everyone has had that icky, annoying experience of walking through a spiderweb face-first. Yet for some reason, spiders can prance across their own webs gleefully. So why don't spiders get caught in their own webs?

According to most spider experts, spiders avoid entrapping themselves because of the nature of spider silk. As a spider spins its web, it releases two types of thread: a sticky kind (snare silk) that is covered with a special glue that adheres to just about everything, and a nonsticky variety (anchor silk). As the crafty spider weaves, it remembers which paths are safe to travel and which are treacherous—apparently, spiders have far better memories than most compulsive liars. And if a memory-challenged spider missteps, most arachnids are equipped with two or three claw-like attachments on each of their feet that help them cling to safe strands as they extricate themselves from their own traps.

Some experts believe that spiders may have a chemical advantage, too. They state that arachnids produce an oily substance that coats their legs and makes them immune to their own glue—but not to the glue of other spiders. Which is why you sometimes see the ironic—and somewhat satisfying—sight of a spider caught in the web of another spider. How's that for a tangled web?

Q Do birds get tired in flight?

A Flight—especially migration—can be an exhausting experience for any bird. Reducing the amount of energy that is spent in the air is the primary purpose of a bird's body structure and flight patterns. Even so, migrating thousands of miles twice a year takes its toll on a bird's body, causing some to lose up to 25 percent of their body weight. How do they keep on truckin'?

Large birds cut energy costs by soaring on thermal air currents that serve to both propel them and keep them aloft, which minimizes the number of times the beasts have to flap their wings. The concept is similar to a moving walkway at an airport: The movement of the current aids birds in making a long voyage faster while expending less energy.

Smaller birds lack the wingspans to take advantage of these currents, but there are other ways for them to avoid fatigue. The thrush, for instance, has thin, pointed wings that are designed to take it great distances while cutting down on the energy expended by flapping. Such small birds also have light, hollow bone structures that keep their body weights relatively low.

If you've ever seen a gaggle of migrating geese, you likely noticed the distinctive V-formation that they take in flight. They do this to save energy. The foremost goose takes the brunt of the wind resistance, while the geese behind it in the lines travel in the comparatively calm air of the leader's wake. Over the course of a migration, these birds rotate in and out of the leader position, thereby dispersing the stress and exhaustion.

While large birds routinely migrate across oceans, smaller birds tend to keep their flight paths over land—they avoid large bodies of water, mountain ranges, and deserts. This enables them to make the occasional pit stop.

Perhaps the most amazing avian adaptation is the ability to take short in-flight naps. A bird accomplishes this by means of unilateral eye closure, which allows it to rest half of its brain while the other half remains conscious. In 2006, a study of Swainson's Thrush—a species native to Canada and some parts of the United States—showed that the birds took hundreds of in-flight naps a day. Each snooze lasted no more than a few seconds, but in total, they provided the necessary rest.

How sweet is that? After all, who among us wouldn't want to take naps at work while still appearing productive?

Q What is the record for the most milk from a cow?

A Number 289 may not have looked like much, but she was a real cash cow. Owned by M. G. Maciel & Son Dairy of Hanford, California (which did not name its animals), number 289 produced 465,224 pounds of milk during her lifetime (1964–1984). How many gallons is that? Get out your calculator.

One gallon of milk weighs about 8.6 pounds. So number 289, a Holstein breed, produced about 54,070 gallons in her lifetime. Given that cows start lactating around age two, that works out to 3,004 gallons a year. To make things a little more complicated, dairy farmers often prefer to measure milk production in lactation cycles, which are ten months long. Using this standard, 289 cranked out 2,503 gallons per cycle.

As you can see, measuring milk is not a simple process. While number 289 may hold the lifetime record, the record for the most milk produced in one year was set by a Holstein named Lucy, of the LaFoster Dairy in North Carolina. In 1998, she produced 75,275 pounds of milk, or roughly twenty-four gallons per day. The previous annual record was held by another Holstein, Ellen, of Fulton County, Indiana; she produced 55,560 gallons in 1973. Ellen's all-time daily high was twenty-three gallons, in January 1975.

The Dairy Herd Improvement Association (DHIA), however, does not recognize number 289 as the all-time champion, because the agency did not record her milk production. The DHIA's champ is Granny, of Koepke Farms Incorporated in Oconomowoc, Wisconsin. Granny produced 458,609 pounds of milk, or about 53,327 gallons, before she died in June 2006 at the age of twenty.

How do these heavyweights compare to the average heifer? According to the DHIA, a healthy dairy cow can produce between 17.4 and 20.9 gallons per day when lactating. For most cows, that's about 305 days per year. Statistics from the U.S. Department of Agriculture reveal that in 2007, an active dairy cow averaged 20,267 pounds of milk. When you consider that dairy cows in 1900 produced fewer than ten thousand pounds annually, you can see that we are living in a land flowing with milk, if not honey.

The 1994 introduction of bovine somatotropin, commonly known as bovine growth hormone (BGH), has no doubt been responsible for some of the surge in milk production. Although there isn't proof that BGH is a health risk for cows or people, its use has sparked considerable controversy. Are champion milk cows that are given BGH the bovine equivalent of human athletes on steroids? That's an issue that can be argued until, well, the cows come home.

Meanwhile, whether you prefer organic or hormonally enhanced milk, you can lift a glass of the white stuff in honor of number 289, who did her thing the old-fashioned way. Like any true champ, her number has been retired back in Hanford.

Q What makes owls so wise?

A The owl is fairly unique among birds. Its eyes are on the front of its head instead of on the sides like most birds. If an owl wants to look sideways, it can turn its head about three-quarters of the way around. However, the trait with which we most commonly associate owls is wisdom. Are owls really all that wise?

Well, it depends on your point of reference. If you're comparing them to other birds, owls do have impressive vision and hunting skills. They fly so quietly that snapped-up mice generally don't know what hit them. But if you talk to wildlife rehabilitators and others who work with owls on a regular basis, "wisdom" and "intelligence" aren't two words you're likely to hear. Other birds, such as crows, are much easier to train.

The owl's reputation comes from its association with Athena, the Greek goddess of wisdom. In one myth, Athena chose the owl as her favorite bird because of its somber appearance and demeanor. Athena was also a warrior, and the owl was viewed as a symbol of protection in battle; if an owl was sighted from the battlefield, it was considered an omen of victory. Because of the link to Athena, owls were considered sacred in ancient Greece. Many Greek coins bear images of owls, and the owl is used to represent Athena herself, in addition to showing up next to her in art and sculpture. Some scholars believe that Athena may have originally been a bird or a bird-like goddess.

In legend and mythology, then, the owl is indeed wise. But in reality, not so much.

Q Why do deer freeze in the headlights?

A It is a universal human moment: You're stunned, confused, and blown into a state of complete disarray, and all you can do is stand there silently and motionlessly. Witnesses agree: You were caught like a deer in the headlights.

We all know what it means, and some of us have even seen the inspiration for this adage firsthand, so the obvious question is why? Why does a deer that is surprised by the lights of an oncoming car freeze in the middle of the road and seem to wait for the impact?

There are a couple of scientific theories concerning this phenomenon. (Neither has anything to do with depression, suicidal tendencies among forest fauna, or a masculine desire to display bravery by playing chicken in traffic.) These theories attribute the animal's reaction to instinct.

According to the first explanation, the deer presumes that anything it doesn't recognize is a predator. It stops moving to reduce the risk of being seen and waits for the predator to move on or give chase. Unfortunately, when the "predator" is a set of vehicle headlights, standing still for any amount of time is a bad idea, and the deer will often wind up as roadkill.

The other theory posits that the deer is temporarily stricken with a sort of blindness that is caused by powerful high-beam headlamps. Since a deer lacks the cognitive ability to understand why the forest, grass, sky, and road have all disappeared, it simply freezes because there's nowhere to go. While the animal is waiting for its sight to be restored...*wham!* Roadkill. If the deer is lucky, its revenge is a totaled hatchback and a stranded commuter. But that's hardly an even score: one dead, one terribly inconvenienced.

If you ever find the road blocked by a frozen deer, there are some ways to get the animal moving again. Blinking your lights, flashing your brights, or honking your horn will often startle the deer into movement. Don't attempt to swerve around the animal; this may spin you out of control and into oncoming traffic or the nearest tree. Instead, hit the brakes while doing the aforementioned blinking, flashing, and/or honking, and hope that the deer comes to its senses. Otherwise—*wham!*—it'll be roadkill.

Q Do animals keep harems?

A We aren't the only ones who keep harems. Plenty of animals do, too—and for good reasons.

Humans first: The stereotypical harem was brought to the Western world's attention by the Ottoman Empire, which ruled much of the Middle East and southeast Europe from the thirteen hundreds until the end of World War I. The Imperial Harem of the sultan was guarded by eunuchs and could house more than a thousand women, more than enough for one man.

Animals, however, were keeping harems long before the Ottoman Empire existed. Animals fall into several different basic mating categories. There are the monogamous animals, like wolves and eagles (and a seemingly small percentage of humans), which mate with one partner for life. There are the promiscuous creatures, like chimpanzees, which mate with pretty much any other of their kind at any time. And then there are the harem-keepers, or the polygamists; in these cases, a male mates with several females (polygyny) or a female mates with several males (polyandry). Monogamy is actually rare in the animal world—most animals prefer polygamy or promiscuity.

Perhaps the most famous harem-keepers are social insects such as ants and bees. Harems, however, come in all shapes and sizes. One study conducted in the wild animal reserves of Ghana concluded that animals that keep harems are less likely to become extinct than monogamous creatures. This could be due to a number of factors. For one, hunters tend to take more males than females, leaving fewer males as mating partners. It's also easier for a hunter to sneak up on a pair or a small group than on a large harem. Another benefit of harems may be genetic diversity: The more males with whom a female mates, the more diverse the offspring, which increases the chances of the species surviving new diseases and other threats.

Finally, spare a thought for asexual animals, which reproduce without sex. Although these generally are single-celled organisms, their ranks also include more advanced animals such as Komodo dragons and geckos. Pity these poor beasts. Keeping harems, after all, seems like a lot more fun.

Q Why are bulls enraged by the color red?

A Red has been the color of choice of bullfighters for centuries. Their bright-red capes are used to incite their bovine opponents into spectacular rages. In fact, the phrase "seeing red" is believed to have originated from the fury that the color seems to provoke in the bull. What is it about red that ticks off bulls?

The truth is: nothing. Bulls are partially color-blind and don't respond to the color red at all. The red color of the cape is just eye candy for the audience, much like the bullfighter's *traje de luces* (suit of lights).

Then is it the motion of the cape that infuriates the bull? The truth is: no. There's nothing that the matador does that makes the bull angry—it's in ill humor before it even enters the ring. These bulls aren't bred to take quiet walks in the park on Sunday afternoons. No, they are selected because they exhibit violent and aggressive behavior. By the time they hit the bullfighting arena, just about anything will set them off.

We're talking about bulls that have personalities like John McEnroe. The color red doesn't make them angry—*everything* makes them angry. Then again, the bullfighter plunging his sword into the bull's neck might have something to do with the beast's nasty disposition, too.

Q Will a shark die if it quits moving?

A In the movie *Annie Hall*, Woody Allen's character, Alvy Singer, says: "A relationship, I think, is like a shark, you know? It has to constantly move forward or it dies. And I think what we got on our hands is a dead shark." This may be true of Woody Allen's relationships, but is it true of sharks?

For most sharks, no. But some species—affectionately known as obligate ram ventilators to marine biologists—must indeed keep forging ahead or they will drown.

Like other fish, sharks breathe using gills, which are essentially collections of blood vessels. As water rushes by the gills, the blood absorbs oxygen molecules that are dissolved in the water and expels carbon dioxide molecules. Water doesn't have a ton of absorbable oxygen to go around, so fish need to continually keep water moving past their gills in order to breathe.

Most fish have a simple muscular pumping system that lets them take in water through the mouth and push it past the gills. This is the way to do it if you're going to spend a lot of time in one spot, like most fish.

But sharks are not like most fish. Some breathe primarily through ram ventilation—water rushes in through their mouths and past their gills as they zip along from feeding frenzy to feeding frenzy. Most shark species also have a secondary built-in pump system, so they can take an occasional breather, if you will.

But some sharks, including the infamous great white, lost this backup pump system during their evolution. Basically, they developed a lifestyle that keeps them on the move constantly, and the pumping system became obsolete.

Of course, sharks seldom stop to smell the sea roses, and few marine bullies would dare to hold one still until it drowned, so dying because of a lack of movement is rarely an issue.

Q Why do firehouses keep Dalmatians?

A A great debate rages over whether the Dalmatian hails from Egypt, Asia, or Dalmatia (which is a region in Eastern Europe that is largely situated in Croatia), for which the dog is named.

Luckily, we don't have to answer that question. We've been charged with telling you how Dalmatians wound up in firehouses, which is a comparatively easy assignment.

Dalmatians are hardworking, sensitive, and fiercely loyal dogs that have great memories and a passion for running and hunting vermin. They're also quite social—they become lonely and depressed without regular interaction. In addition to forming strong bonds with their human owners, they get along famously with horses, on which they have a calming effect.

Based on these traits, Dalmatians were trained and used in England, Scotland, and Wales as "coach dogs" by the seventeen hundreds. The horse-drawn carriage was the main mode of transport at the time, and the coach dog ran under or beside the carriage, occasionally speeding ahead to clear other dogs or people out the way for the horses.

Furthermore, Dalmatians guarded the carriage and horses when the master was away. In an age when horse thievery was common, a stagecoach driver with a Dalmatian could afford the luxury of sleeping in a hotel room rather than with the coach and horses, since he knew that his trusty dog would sound its *woof-woof* alarm if anyone disturbed the carriage.

Fire departments of this era also relied on horses to pull their specially equipped wagons. Enter Dalmatians, which cleared traffic as the wagons sped to a fire. Once there, the dogs kept the horses calm and the equipment safe while the firefighters did their jobs.

Dalmatians performed their duties equally well at American firehouses, but their gig ended when engine-powered fire trucks rolled onto the scene in the first part of the twentieth century. Now Dalmatians are relegated to the role of mascot in fire departments in England, the United States, and Canada—a symbolic nod to the rough-hewn days when blazes weren't fought without them.

Q Can animals tell time?

A Have you ever noticed your dog eying you expectantly when it's time for its dinner or daily walk? Animals do seem to have an instinct for knowing how long it's been since their last meal or walk.

And research suggests that on some level, animals can indeed tell time. But can they grasp time as an abstract concept, as we do? Humans can comprehend that something occurred at a specific time in the last few hours, or days, or years—but can animals?

A 2008 study at the University of Western Ontario in Canada found that rats can remember how long ago something happened, but they can't mentally travel back to the specific point when that something happened. This is called episodic-like memory, or what-when-where memory. Humans have this ability, but they also have associated emotions and other knowledge relative to the remembered experience, which is called episodic memory.

A different study on animal memory, conducted in 1998, showed that scrub-jays remembered where they hid different types of food, and that the birds retrieved it depending on the amount of time that had elapsed and the perishable nature of the edibles. This seemed to be a clear example of episodic memory: The scrub-jays appeared to remember where they put something and when they put it there.

However, William A. Roberts, the psychologist who conducted the University of Western Ontario study, argues that the scrub-jay experiment was not an example of episodic memory at all. Instead, he says, the birds were simply keeping track of how much time had passed since they hid their items.

What is the general consensus among scientists about animal memory? There isn't one at the moment. Suffice it to say, animals tell time, but not in the same way that humans do.

Q Can cats suffocate babies by taking away their breath?

A No, but that doesn't make the myth any less interesting. Its origin may lie with the legend of the succubus, a demonic nocturnal spirit, usually feminine, that sucks life from its victims. With their eerie eyes, night-stalking habits, and association with witches, cats fit the succubus profile.

Before much was known about sudden infant death syndrome (SIDS), a person who discovered a cat close to a dead baby might have been quick to assume that the feline had something to do with it. In 1791, a coroner in Plymouth, England, ruled that a cat killed a child by sucking the child's breath. The report does not mention evidence that may have been gathered to support this conclusion.

On December 21, 2000, Nicola Payne of London found her six-week-old son dead in·his crib with the family cat curled up next to him. The media reported that the cat had suffocated the baby by lying on his face. But an investigation did not reveal cat hair in the infant's nose, mouth, or airways: Pathologists concluded that SIDS was the cause.

Indeed, there are no verifiable cases of cats causing infant deaths. However, cats are attracted to warm, cozy places like cribs, so veterinarians and pediatricians recommend that newborn babies and cats be kept apart when an adult is not present. A cat may be aroused by the scent of milk on a baby's breath and attempt to explore the source of the odor. Or it may mistake a baby's crying for the mewing of a rival feline and become aggressive.

With a little common sense and patience, cats and tots can get along just fine, as millions of happy feline-owning parents can verify.

Q Are pigs pigs?

A Poor pigs—they are so misunderstood. No creature is thought of in the popular mind in such diametric opposites. On one hand, you have the lovable, heroic Babe from the film of the same name, and the gentle, simple Wilbur from the classic children's novel *Charlotte's Web*. On the other, you have the pig as it exists in the English language—when we are gluttonous, we "eat like pigs"; when we perspire unpleasantly, we "sweat like pigs." And, of course, many women will attest that a certain percentage of men "behave like pigs."

So which is it? Are pigs gentle and lovable or slovenly and lascivious? It depends on whom you ask. Despite the pig's low standing in the American consciousness, pigs have been honored for thousands of years in other cultures. In China, pigs were considered a symbol of prosperity and are honored as one of the twelve signs of the Chinese zodiac. In the Hindu religion, the god Vishnu appeared as a pig to save the world. And in both ancient Egypt and ancient Greece, pigs were sacrificed to honor the gods.

Zoologists have many good things to say about pigs. According to pig experts, the *Sus domestica,* as the pig is called in scientific circles, is one of the smartest domesticated creatures on the planet and, contrary to popular belief, one of the cleanest. Indeed, if left to their own devices, pigs will maintain a clean, organized living space and will go outside to a designated toilet area when they need to relieve themselves. (So women who call men "pigs" might be giving men a little too much credit.)

Still, this doesn't stop people from making ugly pig comparisons. Pig apologists point out that many of these insulting phrases are rooted in misunderstandings. "Sweating like a pig," for example, makes no sense whatsoever, as pigs don't have sweat glands. However, this trait may be one reason why pigs have obtained their reputation for slovenliness—pigs use mud to cool and protect themselves on hot days (the source of the phrase "happy as a pig in slop"), so they seem to be filthy creatures, at least to those who are unaware of the circumstances.

So the next time someone tells you that you're acting like a pig, feel free to respond by regaling the person with some piggy truth. Keep it short and sweet, though, or you might get called a bore instead.

Q When do fish sleep?

A It's hard to tell whether fish are sleeping because they don't have eyelids. That's why you'll never win a staring contest with your pet goldfish—its eyes are always open.

So how do fish get their beauty sleep? They don't, at least not in the way we humans do. Their body functions slow down and they get a bit dozy, but they're generally still alert enough to scatter when danger arises. You could say that they're having a relaxing daydream, but they never actually fall into a deep sleep.

Some fish simply float motionless in the water as they doze; others, such as grouper and rockfish, rest against rocks or plants. The craftier varieties, like bass and perch, hole up underneath rocks and logs or hide in crevices. Others stay on the move while in a daze, recharging without ever stopping.

In the 1930s, biologist David Graham watched a fish sleeping upright on its tail for an hour or so. Then Graham turned on the lights, and the fish jerked back into a swimming position and darted around. It was the aquatic equivalent of being caught napping in school.

When exactly do fish rest? It varies from species to species. Most fish rely on the weak light from the surface to see, and since that light pretty much disappears at night, it's thought that a lot of fish do their resting then. However, some fish rest during the day, while others do so randomly. There are, it seems, no set bedtimes in the fish world.

Chapter Six

BODY SCIENCE

Q Why does reading in the car make you sick?

A The theory goes that motion sickness is a physical response to a perceived paradox; in other words, it's your body saying, "This does not compute." Conflicting information is transmitted by separate receptors: One says that you're moving, while the other says that you're not. Your stomach winds up being the loser of the debate, and the results can include nausea and vomiting.

Your body has various methods of determining its position and state of motion. One is a set of receptors in the inner ear that controls your balance. When fluid inside the cochlea moves, it stimulates the tiny hairs that grow there. The movement of these hairs notifies your brain when you are listing to the left, tilting to the right, or leaning into a powerful wind. These hairs also detect when your body is in motion. The eyes comprise another set of receptors that is important to establishing motion. When you see trees flying by on either side, you can be pretty sure that it is your body that is moving and not the forest.

When you read in the car (or play a handheld video game or look at a map for an extended time), your gaze is focused on a fixed point. According to the stimuli that are recorded by your visual receptors, your body is at rest. "But, no!" protests your inner ear. "Of course we're still moving!" The tiny hairs, which sway as you bump and jostle, send the message of movement to the brain.

Faced with this paradox, the brain overloads. Dizziness ensues; the stomach is upset; and, if it's a severe case, lunch is lost. And it's all because of an argument between two stubborn sensory receptors, neither of which will admit to being wrong.

Fortunately, motion sickness is common enough to warrant readily available medication that can prevent the nausea from taking hold in the first place. But what if you don't take any medication before settling into the backseat of a car and reading this compelling book? If you start to feel queasy, raise your eyes from these pages and look at the horizon. Showing your eyes that, yes, you are indeed moving will settle both the argument and, eventually, your stomach.

That is, until you start reading again. The eyes are forgetful little beasts—they'll soon return to thinking that you are standing still, and the debate will rage all over again.

Q How long can you live without sleep?

A Nobody knows for certain, but Dr. Nathaniel Kleitman, the father of modern sleep research, said: "No one ever died of insomnia." Still, what doesn't kill you can still have some nasty side effects.

Various studies have revealed that missing just one night of sleep can lead to memory loss and decreased activity in certain parts of the brain. So if you're planning an all-night cram session for the evening before the big mid-term, you may be better off closing the book and getting a good night's sleep.

Then again, maybe not. Each person's body and brain handle sleep deprivation differently. Some folks are all but useless after one night without shut-eye, while others function normally. It's largely a matter of biology.

Take Tony Wright. In May 2007, the forty-three-year-old British gardener kept himself awake for 226 hours. He said that he was aiming for the world's sleeplessness record and wanted to prove that sleep deprivation does not diminish a person's coherence. Wright admitted to some odd sensory effects during his marathon, but he insisted that his mental faculties were not compromised.

Wright's quest didn't amount to much more than a lot of lost sleep. *Guinness World Records* stopped acknowledging feats of insomnia in 1990 after consulting with experts at the British Association for Counseling and Psychotherapy. The experts believe that sleep deprivation threatens psychological and physical well-being. Muscle spasms, reduced reaction times, loss of motivation, hallucinations, and paranoia can all be triggered by sleep deprivation. That Wright apparently didn't suffer any of these ill effects doesn't mean you won't. Sometimes, it seems, you lose if you don't snooze.

Q Why do men have more body hair than women?

A First, we need to know what body hair is and isn't. Body—or androgenic—hair begins to grow at the onset of puberty. It includes underarm hair, pubic hair, facial hair, and that soft peach-fuzz hair—also known as vellus hair—around and about your body that becomes dark and thick. Androgenic hair does not include the hair on your head.

Androgenic hair is produced by androgens. What's an androgen? Well, it's not *Saturday Night Live*'s not-really-feminine-or-masculine Pat. An androgen is a hormone, which is a naturally occurring substance in the body. Different types of endocrine glands produce and secrete different types of hormones; they are transmitted via the bloodstream to organs in order to regulate a wide range of biological activities. These hormones include the sex steroids: estrogen, progesterone, and good old androgens. Both men and women have androgens, but they're much more plentiful in guys. (The best-known androgen is testosterone.)

The job of androgens is to bring about the development of male characteristics, such as a deep voice, large muscles, and body hair. When puberty gets the green flag, sex-steroid production shifts into high gear. Girls and boys develop androgenic hair, but boys develop a lot more of it, simply because they have a lot more androgens.

Obviously, men have varying amounts of androgens—some guys look like they're wearing wool sweaters, while others couldn't grow a beard if their lives depended on it. By the time puberty reaches the finish line, androgens have not only separated the men from the boys, but also distinguished the men from the women.

Q Can a person remain conscious after being beheaded?

A No, and yes. A person can't remain conscious long enough to plan and exact revenge on the executioners, but it seems that a severed head can get in a final thought or two.

There are many fantastic stories of living, angry heads from the heyday of decapitation. Charlotte Corday, who was executed in 1793 for the assassination of French radical leader Jean-Paul Marat, reportedly blushed when the executioner slapped her severed head. The heads of two rivals in the French National Assembly allegedly spent their last seconds biting each other. And legend has it that when the executioner held aloft the heart of just-decapitated Sir Everard Digby, a conspirator in the Gunpowder Plot of 1605, and said, "Here lies the heart of a traitor," Digby's head mouthed, "Thou liest."

These are extremely tall tales, but more recent accounts are fairly credible. The most famous is from a French physician named Dr.

Beaurieux, who witnessed the execution of a criminal named Languille in 1905. Beaurieux wrote:

"The face relaxed, the lids half closed on the eyeballs, leaving only the white of the conjunctiva visible. It was then that I called in a strong, sharp voice: 'Languille!' I saw the eyelids slowly lift up, without any spasmodic contractions—I insist advisedly on this peculiarity—but with an even movement, quite distinct and normal, such as happens in everyday life, with people awakened or torn from their thoughts. Next Languille's eyes very definitely fixed themselves on mine and the pupils focused themselves. I was not, then, dealing with the sort of vague dull look without any expression, that can be observed any day in dying people to whom one speaks: I was dealing with undeniably living eyes which were looking at me."

As horrific as this possibility seems, it is biologically feasible. The brain can still function as long as it receives oxygen delivered via blood. While the trauma of the final cut and sudden drop in blood pressure would likely cause fainting, there still would be enough blood available to make consciousness possible. Exactly how much consciousness isn't clear, but the likely cap is about fifteen seconds.

The next logical question is, what might the beheaded be thinking in these final seconds? Here's a possibility: "Ouch!"

Q Do black pants make your butt look smaller?

A This is a tried-and-true trick for those who are a little self-conscious about the junk in their trunks. The good news is, it works a lot better than tying a sweater around your waist or wearing a loud hat to divert attention.

Why is black slimming? One of the main ways we gauge something's size is by analyzing its illumination. In other words, the visual-processing part of the brain figures out something's shape by picking up on patterns of light and shadow.

If the sun is shining on a big butt in yellow pants, the eye takes in a wealth of light and shadow information, giving the brain plenty to analyze. Using this data, the brain can make a dead-on estimate of the shape, size, and general grandeur of the backend in question. But stuff that big butt into black pants, which absorb light more effectively, and there isn't much shadow information with which to work. Without these cues, the brain can't get a good read on the situation—it assumes that the butt is smaller than it really is. Note, however, that this only works when looking at the butt straight on; in profile, the size is obvious.

Dark clothes also do a better job of hiding fabric patterns that provide a sense of shape. If you're wearing jeans, for example, the lines of the seams and back pockets give clues to the shape of your rear. Generally, seams are hidden more effectively on darker trousers.

But remember, black pants can only do so much. They aren't a license to add jelly doughnuts to every meal.

Q Why can't you tickle yourself?

A If only bullies chose this question instead of the far more popular, "Why are you hitting yourself?" You can't tickle yourself because your brain couldn't care less about your attempts at tickling—it basically says, "Duh, I know! I told your fingers to do that." When someone else tickles you, however, the contact is unexpected, and the shock contributes to the effect.

When the nerves of your skin register a touch, your brain responds differently depending on whether you're responsible for it. MRI scans show that three parts of the brain—the secondary somatosensory cortex, the anterior cingulated cortex, and the cerebellum—react strongly when the touch comes from an external source. Think of it like this: When you see a scary movie for the first time, you jump when the maniac suddenly appears and kills the high school kids as punishment for having teenage sex. The second time you see the movie, it isn't a surprise, so you don't jump. The same goes for tickling: It's the element of surprise that causes the giddy laughter of the ticklish.

Why do we laugh hysterically when other people tickle us? Scientists believe that it's an instinctual defense mechanism—an exaggerated version of the tingle that goes up your spine when an insect is crawling on you. This is your body's way of saying, "You may want to make sure whatever is touching you won't kill you." The laughter is a form of panic due to sensory overload.

If you're in desperate need of tickling but have no friends or family willing to help, you can invest in a tickling robot. People do respond to self-initiated remote-control tickling by a specialized robot that was developed by British scientists in 1998. There's a short delay between the command to tickle and the actual tickle, which is enough to make the contact seem like a surprise to the brain and induce fits of laughter.

Now that the pressing problem of alleviating loneliness through robotic tickling has been addressed, scientists can shift their attention back to finding a cure for cancer.

Q Does fear have a smell?

A It's not so much that fear has a smell—fear is an emotion, not a substance—but that humans produce a smell when they're afraid. And we're not just talking about a smell that indicates a need for a clean pair of underwear.

The heart beats faster, breathing kicks into high gear, and a rush of adrenaline might bring on shakiness, all of which cause a person to sweat. The body has special sweat glands for these sorts of occasions. The apocrine glands—concentrated in specific areas, including your armpits and crotch—release a mixture of sweat and bacterial excretions through hair follicles, which yields the smell we know and don't love: B.O.

But don't feel bad. Fear-motivated body odor is produced by many animals, including cats, dogs, mice, rats, and maybe even monkeys. And it could be worse—at least you don't create the stink that a skunk does when it's afraid. Body odor, particularly in the case of skunks, can work as a defense mechanism, sending a primal signal to a potential predator that you're alarmed and you mean business.

Humans are more than equipped to pick up on that signal, since we have two systems that activate the sense of smell. One picks up airborne scent molecules for analysis in the nose. The second system uses the vomeronasal organ that is found on either side of the nasal septum. This organ, it seems, is tied closely to the part of the brain that processes emotions, and it reacts to pheromones, or chemical signals, that are secreted by other humans. In other words, the vomeronasal organ can help you sense when another human is fearful.

What if you smell fear—or anything else, for that matter—and you, in turn, become scared? Then you suffer from olfactophobia, the fear of smell. And your problems are far too complex to be addressed in these humble pages.

Q What are the legal ways to dispose of a body?

A Grandpa's gone, and for some people, the most pressing issue is whether to request a pillow in his coffin. For others, the question is not whether Gramps needs head support, but whether his earthly remains should be buried, cremated, frozen, or perhaps, in the not-too-distant future, liquefied.

Humans are the only creatures known to bury their dead in a systematic way. It's a practice that could date back some hundred thousand years or more, and today's most commonly legal method of burial involves a casket. In the United States, about 80 percent of the deceased are laid in a casket and buried. More than half are displayed in an open casket prior to burial; the rest bow out with the lid shut.

Cremation is the second-most popular method of disposal. Cremation reduces the average-size adult to eight pounds of ash and fragments. The remains typically are kept by loved ones in a small container or scattered in a location of special significance to the deceased. The ashes of *Star Trek* creator Gene Roddenberry, for example, were dispersed in outer space.

Cryonic suspension is another legal way to go, though it is far less common than burial or cremation. Also known as solid-state hypothermia, cryonic suspension involves freezing and maintaining a human body in the hope that scientific advances someday will make it possible to resuscitate the deceased. The corpse is frozen and stored at –321 degrees Fahrenheit, which is the boiling point of liquid nitrogen. Going the frozen route requires lots of cold cash: Cryopreservation can cost as much as $150,000, depending on the level of services one selects. Baseball great Ted Williams awaits his next turn at bat at a cryonic facility in Scottsdale, Arizona.

The volunteering of corpses for organ donation or for medical or scientific research is also gaining popularity. It's the only way that many people ever get into medical school.

Alkaline hydrolysis might be the future of legal body disposal. The process involves placing a body in a steel chamber that contains lye that is heated to three hundred degrees Fahrenheit and is pressurized to sixty pounds per square inch. Think of it as being boiled in acid. The remains are a liquid that can be poured down a drain. Alkaline hydrolysis is currently performed only in a couple of research hospitals in the United States, but there is growing support to make this environmentally friendly method of body disposal available through funeral homes.

As for illegal ways to get rid of a body, you need neither scientists nor undertakers. Guys with names like Big Nicky are the experts in this field; cross them or their cronies, and a body might end up "sleeping with the fishes."

Q What's so funny about your funny bone?

A It's happened to all of us. You're walking a bit too quickly around a corner, and *bam!* You smash your elbow on the corner of a table. And seemingly every time it happens, some stooge is standing right there and says with a chuckle, "Oh, did you hit your funny bone?" As you're seized by a sensation akin to thousands of pins piercing your arm, it takes everything good inside of you not to scream, "No, I hit my '@#+! you' bone!"

The funny bone is the most misnamed part of the body—and not just because of "@#+! you" situations like the one just described. Truth is, the funny bone isn't even a bone; it's a nerve—one of three main nerves in the arm. Called the ulnar nerve, it passes under the collarbone and along the inside of the upper arm, through a tunnel of tissue at the elbow, under the muscles on the inside of the forearm, and into the palm of the hand on the side with the little finger.

The nerve goes around a bump at the elbow called the medial epicondyle. There's a slight groove in the bone where the nerve fits; since the groove is shallow, the nerve sits unusually close to the surface. With so little protection, it can be easily dinged.

Some say that the sensation associated with this ding is painful. Others call it prickly. Still others think that the feeling is funny in a peculiar sort of way—but that's not why it's called the funny bone. What's so funny about it, then? Well, the elbow connects three bones: the radius, the ulna, and the humerus. That's right, humerus, as in humorous. As in people think it's humorous that you smacked your funny bone on the corner of a table.

The ulnar nerve wasn't meant to be comic relief. In addition to providing feeling to the little finger and half of the ring finger, the ulnar nerve controls many of the muscles in the hand that aid with fine movements, as well as some of the bigger gripping muscles in the forearm. Sound funny to you? We didn't think so.

Q Why can't people sneeze with their eyes open?

A Sneezing carries both germs and myths. One such old wives' tale is that you can't sneeze with your eyes open. The truth is, you can—it just takes some effort.

When an irritant touches the nasal mucosa, it sets off the brain's response: sneezing. The sneeze will expel the irritant, clear the nasal and sinus cavities, and—because of the deep inhalation and exhalation of breath—increase the amount of oxygen in the body's cells. There's no specific reason why we close our eyes when this happens. Since a sneeze uses muscles in the face, chest, and abdomen, and since the nerves around the nose and eyes are interconnected, it seems to be a full-body reflex, the blink of the eyes included. But as with other reflexes, it's possible to control the blinking of your eyes while sneezing. Preparation is the key: If you feel a sneeze coming on, you need to focus on not closing your eyes.

Some people make an effort to keep their eyes open if they're about to sneeze when they're driving. But this is a somewhat pointless exercise because the amount of time your eyes are closed during a sneeze is barely longer than a blink. The real danger comes from the sneeze itself, which features an upper-body spasm that can jerk the arms and cause a person to inadvertently move the steering wheel.

There are other dangers associated with sneezing. Stifling a sneeze to avoid making a noise can cause your eardrum to rupture. By keeping your mouth closed—especially if you also hold your nose—you are forcing air to find another way out, and the closest escape is through your Eustachian tube, which leads to the ear.

So if someone gives you the business because of your loud, obnoxious sneeze, simply respond that you're protecting the health of your eardrums. And if the person inquires about why you kept your eyes open? Say it's a new trick you taught yourself.

Q Is it possible to have the crap scared out of you?

A It's rare, but—oh yes—it happens. What would cause someone to soil himself or herself from fear? Evolution. But before you go leafing through your copy of *The Origin of Species* looking for the pants-crapping chapter, allow us to explain.

Humans, like all animals, respond to danger with what is known as the "fight or flight" response. This series of biological reactions from the autonomic nervous system enables us to duke it out or, if overmatched, head for the hills and live to fight another day.

Fight or flight was a literal lifesaver when our ancient ancestors had to decide whether or not to go toe to claw with a mountain lion, but it's less useful for contemporary dangers, such as getting caught looking at Internet porn on your office computer. Either way, an unfortunate by-product is the tendency to void one's bowels in moments of extreme terror.

As your nervous system prepares you to fight or flee, some of the body's attributes are augmented while others are suppressed. For example, heart rate and lung activity increase, while production in the tear ducts and salivary glands shuts down. To achieve this effect, blood vessels that feed these body parts expand or contract, so the blood vessels leading to the muscles in your legs dilate in preparation for exertion. It might seem as if it would be more difficult to fight or flee with a gigantic load in your pants, but this is an evolutionary reflex that predates clothing.

It looks like we have inadvertently answered another timeless head-scratcher: Do bears . . . uh . . . relieve themselves in the woods? You bet they do! Especially if they see a bigger, meaner bear coming at them, ready to kick some bear ass.

Q Why do you get bloodshot eyes after smoking pot?

A Remember that creative writing teacher you had in college who always wore sunglasses to class? No, he wasn't just cool and artsy. He was probably trying to conceal his red eyes, which would have been a dead giveaway that he had burned through a quarter-ounce of marijuana before setting off to mold young minds.

While many people are familiar with the side effects of smoking pot—e.g., heroic appetites for salty snacks and the music of Pink Floyd—few people understand them. So let's examine why good old Mary Jane gives you bloodshot eyes.

When marijuana is inhaled, it has a number of physiological effects. Your heart rate increases and dopamine floods your brain, creating a feeling of euphoria, or being "high." And the blood vessels in the eyes expand, causing them to appear bloodshot. Simple as that.

Of course, there are many other causes of bloodshot eyes. Allergies, dry air, and dust can all irritate the blood vessels in your eyes and cause them to dilate, making them visible on the surface. What you might not know is that the same remedies that you use to clear up irritated and allergic eyes will also work on your peepers after taking seven bong hits.

Products like Visine contain vasoconstrictors that shrink the blood vessels in your eyes, allowing you to walk past your parents with impunity after burning a J in your girlfriend's garage. It should be noted, however, that repeated use of these products can cause a condition called "rebound redness," in which your eyes immediately return to a bloodshot state after the vasoconstrictor wears off.

Right about now, our conscience is forcing us to point out that you shouldn't use illegal drugs—but at least you now know one of the ways they trash your body.

Q Why do we have ear wax?

A What's that you say? Why do we wear slacks? If you are not hearing well, you may have a buildup of cerumen—the medical term for ear wax—in your ears.

Ear wax is produced in the outer ear canal, which is the tunnel between the externally visible part of the ear and the inner ear and is where the eardrum is found. The skin of the outer ear canal uses sweat glands to produce two types of ear wax: "dry" wax (which is gray and flakey) and "wet" wax (gooey and brown). Both are equally effective at their jobs—wet wax just has more lipids, or fatty substance.

So what exactly is the job of ear wax? First, it keeps the skin of the ear moist; if we didn't have ear wax, the dry skin inside the ear would be unbearably itchy. Second, it helps prevent infection; ear wax has antibacterial qualities, and it keeps certain fungi from wreaking havoc on our ears. And third, ear wax traps invaders such as dirt and dust, which might otherwise bust up the joint; think of ear wax as the bouncer at the bar that is your inner ear.

As your ear produces new wax, the old wax is pushed out and is deposited onto your outer ear. The old wax either falls off or is rinsed off when you bathe. Doctors beg us not to stick cotton swabs, keys, knitting needles, or ice picks into our ears to clean them—the wax can take care of itself without our help. Sticking things into your ears is likely to push the cerumen deeper and compact it. You might even puncture your inner ear, which is an extremely painful experience that isn't recommended.

Some people produce excessive wax that needs to be removed; too much of the stuff can cause hearing problems and infection. Older people, in particular, tend to suffer from wax buildup, partly because of hair growth in their ears. If you are a candidate for wax removal, let the experts handle it—they'll coax out that burdensome wax using water, mineral oils, and/or syringes. These tools work a lot better, and are much less hazardous, than the pencil that's sitting on your desk.

Q Why can't we remember much of anything that happened to us before the age of three?

A To spare us the horrific memories of constantly soiling our diapers? Laugh if you will, but Sigmund Freud actually offered an explanation along these lines. Freud, ever the ray of sunshine, believed that we repress our earliest memories because they're uniformly traumatic. (What exactly did this guy's parents do to him?)

Of course, subsequent scientists have had little use for Freud—they've forwarded theories of their own. One post-Freud analysis suggested that young children simply lack the internal equipment to form long-term memories; the prefrontal cortex and hippo-campus—the memory centers of the brain—aren't yet developed enough.

Later studies have demonstrated that it's not that simple. Small children actually *do* have the ability to form lasting memories. A 1994 study, for example, found that 63 percent of twenty-three-month-olds could recall events that they experienced at eleven months. (These tiny tots couldn't talk, of course, so the experiment was designed to teach them a unique series of actions and then see if they could still perform them a year later.) This study, and others like it, show that we have the ability to form long-term memories before we can even talk.

In fact, talking is where the trouble begins. According to some studies, the memory starts working differently once language kicks in. Scientists in New Zealand conducted an experiment to observe memory formation in children who were just learning to talk. When the subjects were two or three years old, with limited language skills, they were exposed to a memorable stimulus: a machine that appeared to shrink big toys into smaller toys. (Don't get excited—it was just an illusion.)

The researchers followed up with the kids later, when their language abilities had further developed. While many of them remembered the mysterious machine, they could only describe it using words and actions that were in their repertoire at the time of their exposure to it. Even though they had developed a greater vocabulary that would have allowed them to describe the magical machine with more clarity, they didn't use these words.

This suggests that our early memories become inaccessible because of a change in the way we think. Before we can talk, our worlds—and our memories—are based solely on disconnected impressions of images and sound. As we learn to talk, we develop the ability to tell stories and the ability to structure our impressions into cohesive plots that become narrative, or "autobiographical," memories. While we're learning to talk, we have access to our pre-language memories, but we can't translate them to fit with our new way of thinking. Pre-verbal memories aren't reinforced by and connected to the narrative memories, so they gradually disappear into thin air.

The lesson? Don't bother dropping thousands of dollars on the big Disney World trip before your kid can talk and can remember it.

Q Why are you born with tonsils if you don't need them?

A We may not *need* tonsils, but they're pretty useful nonetheless. Tonsils are part of the lymphatic system, which is a major component of the all-important immune system. The immune system, of course, is what hunts down and destroys or disarms the various harmful viruses and bacteria that infect our body.

Tonsils are designed to trap germs that come in through your nose and mouth. They also produce antibodies and immune cells that break down and get rid of those sneaky germs. So you shouldn't be in any hurry to remove them.

However, like everything else in the human body, tonsils aren't completely invincible. They can get infected themselves, resulting in swelling, infection, and general painful, oozy unpleasantness. Beyond the pain, this swelling can cause breathing problems, especially in younger children whose tonsils are already quite large in relation to their throats.

Nowadays, doctors don't like to remove tonsils without plenty of justification. But if you do need to have your tonsils taken out, don't fret too much. Going under the knife usually won't lead to any adverse long-term effects, since tonsils are too small a part of the lymphatic system to make a massive difference in your overall health. Your body can manage without them; it's very well designed. Still, if your tonsils are not causing you any major problems, just hang on to them and let them do their germ-fighting thing. It can't hurt.

Q Why did they put coins in the eyes of dead people?

A As if death wasn't a big enough downer, it accounts for one of the biggest expenses the average person will ever incur. From caskets to flowers to embalming services, people pay through the nose for a decent burial. And until fairly recently, you could say that the dead also paid through the eyes.

The most common explanation for the tradition of putting coins on the eyes of the dead points to the mythical Greek figure of Charon, one of the Western world's first undertakers. Typically depicted as a morose, somewhat creepy old man (undertakers haven't changed much in three thousand years, apparently), Charon was a ferry- man who conveyed the souls of the dead  to the land of the dead across the rivers Styx and Acheron.

Much like today's undertakers, Charon's services came at a price. The cost of a ride to Hades was an *obol,* an ancient Greek coin valued at one-sixth of a drachma (the equivalent of fifteen to twenty dollars in today's world). Placing the coins on the corpse's eyes, the Charon theory holds, was to ensure that the soul would reach its final destination.

Though this explanation seems convincing, a thorough review of Greek mythology identifies one major flaw in the argument: Charon, who was a picky sort, would only accept payment if the coin was placed in the mouth of the corpse. Hence, the tradition in ancient Greece was to put coins in dead people's mouths, not in their eye sockets.

However, the ancient Greeks were not the only ones who be- lieved that money was necessary in the afterlife. Many civiliza- tions, including the Egyptians and the Incas, buried their dead with money and other treasure to make sure that the deceased were comfortable in eternity. So it is possible that the erroneous attribution to Greek mythology is rooted in fact.

A more likely explanation, though, is a combination of this my-thology and simple practicality. When a human body dies, rigor mortis sets in. One of the more troubling aspects of this condition is the tendency for the eyelids to pop open. Not only is it creepy to have a dead person staring at you, but in many ancient tradi-tions, it was considered bad luck for the dead person to cross into the afterlife with his or her eyes open—the corpse, it was be-lieved, would look for someone to take with it. Coins—which fit nicely into the eye sockets, are weighty enough to counteract the effects of rigor mortis, and could be used as emergency funds at a post-mortem tollbooth—were the ideal solution.

Among some people, the custom of putting coins in the eyes of the dead continued until at least the late nineteenth century, when mortuary scientists figured out how to deal with rigor mortis. Besides, undertakers no longer require payment from the orifices of the dead. Just those of the living.

Q Can you get paralyzed from the waist up?

A For the average person, paralysis from the waist up would be truly disastrous. Not only would you look like you work for the Ministry of Silly Walks, but formerly simple acts like eating, talking, and even breathing would be impossible to accomplish on your own. Worst of all would be the TV situation. How would you operate the remote?

Before we can figure out whether this nightmare scenario is even possible, we need a refresher course on the human nervous system. The most central part of the nervous system is what we usually call—surprisingly enough—the central nervous system, which is made up of the brain and the spinal cord. The brain, of course, is where the action happens. Nerve impulses enter and your brain interprets them as sights, sounds, and sensations. Nerve impulses also exit—these are the commands your brain sends that put the parts of your body in motion. The other piece of your central nervous system, the spinal cord, serves as the conduit for all the signals as they enter and leave the brain.

Because the spinal cord is the link between the brain and the rest of the body, any damage to it is potentially disastrous. Injuries to the spinal cord are a leading cause of paralysis. Depending on what is injured, several types of paralysis are possible. Paraplegia—the most common condition, in which the legs are paralyzed—usually happens as a result of injuries to the lower part of the spine, which is known as the lumbar. A paraplegic retains command of his or her upper body because the nerves that serve those areas leave the spinal cord above the damaged area. But when the injury occurs higher on the spine, the arms and sometimes even the head are also affected; this condition is known as quadriplegia or tetraplegia.

So it may seem as if there is no way you can get paralyzed from the waist up—any damage to your spine that is high enough to affect your arms will necessarily affect your lower extremities as well. But spinal injuries aren't the only potential cause of paralysis.

Until now we've been talking mostly about the central nervous system—the brain and spinal cord. But once the nerves leave the spinal cord, they become part of what we usually call the peripheral nervous system, which is the fine network of nerves that is woven into the tissues of our body. Whenever you taste or touch or feel something, that nerve impulse begins in your peripheral nervous system. Likewise, when your brain sends a command to move the muscles of your body, it's the peripheral nervous system that executes the order.

Some illnesses—especially polio—can cause paralysis by damaging the peripheral nerves that trigger the muscles. Theoretically, an illness could strike only the nerves that affect the arms and torso, rendering a person paralyzed from the waist up. In fact, some cases of such a condition have been reported. Rarely, though, do these illnesses result in total paralysis from the waist up, nor is the paralysis usually permanent.

Q Why do albinos have red eyes?

A Gotcha! The premise is faulty—not all albinos have red eyes. Albinism is an inherited genetic flaw that interferes with the body's production of pigment, or melanin. According to the National Organization for Albinism and Hypopigmentation, the condition affects an estimated one in seventeen thousand Americans, though not all are affected in the same way: Surprise!—the majority of albinos have blue eyes.

For those who do have red eyes, the cause is a lack of pigment in a cell layer outside the retina. Without pigment, light shoots through the eyeball and is reflected from the interior surface, which illuminates the hundreds of miniscule blood vessels that pulse through the eye and gives the eyeball the appearance of having a red shade.

Okay, that sounds kind of gross, but it's similar to what happens when you take a red-eye photograph. In that case, the flash happens too suddenly for the pupil to close; the eye lets in too much light—enough to illuminate the blood vessels—which is why we (and the camera) see red.

One form of albinism, ocular albinism, affects the eyes, but not the skin or hair. With this condition, some boys—and it's almost exclusively boys who get this type of albinism—have blue, gray, or even brown eyes, but their vision is weak. The fovea, an area of the retina, develops incompletely, and the eyes' nerve fibers have quirky routing. For many who have this condition, not even glasses can help—the eyes simply cannot process sharp images.

As for other forms of albinism, various classifications—which result from slightly different defects that hide in recessive genes—are recognized. The International Albinism Center of the University of Minnesota defines two major classifications: ocular albinism (described above) and oculocutaneous albinism, which affects eye, skin, and hair color. The most severe form of albinism produces white hair, pale skin, and red eyes.

Albinism always involves eye problems of some degree due to the missing melanin. Light sensitivity, astigmatism, nearsightedness or farsightedness, nerve misrouting, and eye-muscle problems all can combine to weaken vision in albinos. So, yes, all albinos have issues with their eyes—but redness isn't necessarily one of them.

Chapter Seven

TRADITIONS

Q **Why would anyone buy an aluminum Christmas tree?**

A For the same reason anyone bought cars with fins or transistor radios: The aluminum tree was once the latest high-tech, shiny, groovy gadget.

On a cold and gray Chicago morning in December 1958, Tom Gannon saw a unique, homemade metal tree in a Christmas display at a Ben Franklin five-and-dime discount store. The favorably impressed Gannon was the toy sales manager of the Aluminum Specialty Company of Manitowoc, Wisconsin—and by the following Christmas, his firm had the aluminum Christmas tree on the market. It was a hit. Over the next ten years, Aluminum

Specialty Company sold more than one million Evergleam trees in sizes ranging from two to eight feet tall. At least forty other companies jumped on the bandwagon, and aluminum trees were manufactured through the 1970s.

The trees were modern and flashy. Their metallic sheen complemented any color scheme, and ornaments glittered off the sparkling boughs. They also were reusable—individual branches fit into holes in the trunk, so that when the holidays were over, the whole bundle of holiday cheer could be carefully taken apart and shoved in the attic until next Christmas. There was just one downside: The electrical conductivity of the branches made strands of Christmas lights a no-no. But some owners used rotating floodlights to bathe their trees in different tints as a substitute for that tradition.

So who killed the aluminum Christmas tree? One unlikely suspect is a certain prematurely bald youngster from the funny pages. In 1965, CBS premiered *A Charlie Brown Christmas*. The animated film used a big pink aluminum tree as a symbol of yuletide commercialism and fakery. Was it coincidence that the popularity of aluminum trees took a nosedive soon after? Whatever the cause, suddenly you couldn't give aluminum trees away. Tastes changed, and everyone wanted a natural, sweet-smelling, green Christmas tree. Even fake trees went green.

Today the vintage aluminum models are sought-after collectibles, and nostalgic reproductions of aluminum trees go in and out of fashion. Like fins on cars, aluminum trees evoke a specific era. Those who remember such trees from their childhoods look at them fondly—for about five minutes. Then they wonder, "What was I thinking?"

Q Whatever happened to pink lawn flamingos?

A It stands on thin metal legs, an icon of mid-century booms: the baby boom, the suburbia boom, the home-ownership boom. It's the lawn flamingo.

As upwardly mobile working-class families left crowded cities following World War II to become landed gentry on tidy plots in the suburbs, American popular culture adopted a whimsical new aesthetic. Automobiles sprouted useless fins. Garish vinyl and Formica dinette sets replaced sturdy kitchen tables. And land-scape design eschewed mossy notions of what was proper and dignified. Forward-looking young homeowners embraced moder-nity, adorning their groomed green yards with splashes of color, including the fiery pink plastic flamingo.

Conceived in 1957 by Don Featherstone—a designer at the Union Products lawn-ornament company in Leominster, Massa-chusetts—plastic flamingos were an instant hit. Millions roosted on front lawns from coast to coast.

But the line between trendy and tacky is a fine one, and pink flamingos crossed it in the 1970s. Some housing developments banned them. Pranksters kidnapped them and sent the rightful owners pictures of their purloined birds perched in exotic locales around the globe. Sales were slow into the early 1980s.

Then, like bowling shirts and the Village People, fake flamingos returned as ironically hip kitsch. Union Products was selling as many as two hundred and fifty thousand annually into the 1990s. The company was forced to halt production in 2006, however, because of financial problems and the rising costs of plastic resin and electricity. But in April 2007, another company stepped in and bought the copyright and the molds with the intention of resuming production.

Modernity, kitsch, dementia—there are many explanations for why people have decorated their lawns with fake flamingos. Featherstone offered one to the *New York Times* upon the pink flamingo's fortieth birthday. "We tried to design things for people of taste," he said, "but we found out there were not too many of them. So we went for the flamingos."

Q Did Mother Goose write her own nursery rhymes?

A Should we even point out that geese can't write? Nah, why bother? Mother Goose made her first appearance in literary history way back in 1650 with a bit part in a French book called *La Muse Historique*. The author gave Mother Goose—or *Mere Oye*, as she's called in French—a passing reference in a single line that translates to "like a Mother Goose story." Hardly an auspicious debut for a character who would eventually become so venerable.

But Mother Goose didn't have to wait too long for her big break. Roughly fifty years later, French lawyer and poet Charles Perrault took her name and made it famous. During the reign of Louis XIV, Perrault served as a poet laureate, producing odes to commemorate events in the life of the Sun King. He also wrote love poems, memoirs, essays, short stories, and a book of tales called *Histoires ou contes du temps pass, avec des moralités (Histories or Tales of Past Times, with Mor-als).* The frontispiece of the book carried an engraving of an old woman and the words *Contes de la Mere l'Oye,* which, as you've prob-ably figured out, means "Tales of Mother Goose." Later editions replaced Perrault's original title with the more memorable *Tales of Mother Goose.*

Perrault's stories were fairy tales, not the rhymes with which we associate Mother Goose today. His work included stories about Sleeping Beauty, Little Red Riding Hood, Cinderella, Puss 'n Boots, and others. Perrault published these stories in 1697—more than a century before the Brothers Grimm gathered versions of many of the same folk stories from the German countryside for their own book of fairy tales.

How did Mother Goose get her current association with juvenile poems like "Humpty Dumpty"? In the 1760s, another author, John Newbery, wrote a book of nursery rhymes and called it *Mother Goose's Melody: or Sonnets for the Cradle,* which was published on both sides of the Atlantic. In America, a printer in Boston distributed it. Perhaps that's why, a century later, some folks tried to claim that Mother Goose was a Bostonian matron named Elizabeth Goose, who was related to the printer. But as you now know, this claim was just a fairy tale.

Q Why are you not supposed to wear white after Labor Day?

A All good GRITS (girls raised in the South) know that you're not supposed to wear white after Labor Day—or before Easter Sunday. It's what their mamas taught them. It's a Southern tradition. And in the South, you don't mess with tradition.

Does that mean the no-white rule originated below the Mason-Dixon Line? Fashion etiquette does trend a bit more formal in this section of the United States. It's a region where upbringing, social skills, and unspoken rules have always been central to living the genteel life. And Southern belles know bad manners when they see them.

Just imagine their horror when the nouveau riche in the late nineteenth century began showing up at tea parties and cotillions in the middle of October wearing snowy, milky, unpigmented garments. They probably didn't carry proper parasols either. Oh my.

Though we can't be certain, it is conceivable the no-white-after-Labor-Day rule was an edict handed down by members of long-standing society families. They were quite concerned about the fashion etiquette of those who lacked the experience, finesse, and good taste of old money. So they established specific codified guidelines for the newbies. (By the way, don't even think about wearing velvet after Valentine's Day.)

What's the point of a seasonal style statute? For Southern ladies, it still may be about honoring heritage and showing respect. For the rest of us, it's a simple reminder to put warm-weather fabrics like seersucker and linen away for the winter.

Fashion authorities say it's perfectly okay, if not stylish, to wear white year-round, especially in a temperate climate. Not convinced? Emily Post—the most trusted name in etiquette—says: "The old rule about wearing white only between Memorial Day and Labor Day is a thing of the past. Today the question of wearing white applies to the weight of the fabrics, not color."

So don't wear a white eyelet sundress to Christmas dinner. And please—please!—put away the bright white pumps. Diann Catlin, an etiquette consultant from Jacksonville, Florida, says it's not white clothes that are a no-no after Labor Day—it's white shoes. Whatever the rule, tennis players and brides are exempt.

Q Why is black the color of mourning?

A It's not clear whether black's negative connotations caused it to become associated with mourning, or if its link to mourning caused it to take on those connotations. What is evident is that black's history as the color of mourning is a long one.

The relationship goes back at least as far as the ancient Egyptians. The Roman Empire followed suit, and in later centuries the Roman Catholic Church's color sequence assigned black as a symbol of mourning. Indeed, this somber function feels natural. We seem to instinctively associate black with negativity—think of the dark feelings brought on by the passing of a loved one.

Black, however, isn't inexorably linked to doom and gloom in every society. Asian and some Slavic cultures consider white to be the color of mourning. In Buddhism, white is symbolic of old age and death. Brides in Japan wear white, but in contrast with Western culture, where bridal white is a symbol of purity or joy, a Japanese bride's white robe signifies her "death" from life at home with her parents.

Q Why do the English call a bathroom the "loo"?

A It's just a catchy word, isn't it? A bit namby-pamby, but funny. And we all know that the English love being funny.

The truth is, the origin of the word "loo" is lost in the swirl of toilet history. According to the *Oxford English Dictionary,* the first mention of it was in 1922, in James Joyce's *Ulysses:* "O yes, mon loup. How much cost? Waterloo. Water closet." So maybe Joyce made it up. Or maybe he got it from somewhere else. There are several theories, which we'll present for your edification.

One is that it comes from Waterloo, which was the trade name of a company that was involved in building outhouses in Britain in the early twentieth century. "Waterloo" would have been displayed on cisterns around the country and could have been shortened to "loo." There's a distinct lack of evidence for this one, though.

Perhaps the most popular theory is that it comes from "gardyloo," which medieval servants used to shout before throwing the contents of a chamber pot out of the window and into the street. The phrase came from the French *regardez l'eau,* meaning "watch out for the water." But by the time "loo" popped up, "gardyloo" had long been obsolete.

Yet another possibility—this, too, involving French words—is that "loo" came from a slight mispronunciation of *le lieu,* meaning "the place," which was a euphemism for the toilet. But again, evidence to support this theory is lacking.

It could also be short for Lady Louisa. The unfortunate lady was the wife of an earl in the nineteenth century. The couple was visiting friends in 1867 when pranksters took the name card off Louisa's bedroom door and stuck it on the bathroom door. So followed much hilarity as guests started saying they were "going to Lady Louisa." They shared it with friends, and it eventually spread. But guess what? There's no hard evidence to support this either.

A number of other theories are name-oriented, but they, too, lack conclusive evidence. Until solid documentation presents itself, the loo will be shrouded in mystery in addition to unpleasant odors.

Q Why are fire engines red?

A Give a youngster a box of crayons, ask for a drawing of a fire engine, and watch those little fingers reach for red. Kids know that red is the right color for a fire truck—it's adults who don't always agree.

Precisely why fire engines are red is lost in the smoky recesses of history. Experts from such agencies as the U.S. Fire Administration and the National Fire Protection Association (NFPA) cite theories, but even they admit that no one knows for sure. Most conjecture leads to the nineteenth century, when firefighting in America was an ad hoc pursuit and competition between public, private, and volunteer brigades was fierce. Crews would race each other to a blaze, and the first group on the scene took control. Sometimes it was to secure a claim on any fire-insurance money; often it was just for the glory. The rivalry extended to uniforms and equipment: The brighter and more elaborate, the more prestigious. Not only was red the shade most identified with fire, it was the most regal and expensive color with which to paint the firefighting apparatus. Thus was born a tradition.

Another theory holds that red became the accepted color for safety reasons in the early twentieth century, when most automobiles were black and red was thought to stand out best in traffic. Indeed, the visibility of fire trucks to other motorists remains a matter of grave importance. NFPA records show a steady increase in the number of collisions involving fire-emergency vehicles going to or from a blaze. In 2006, for instance, there were 16,020 such collisions, resulting in 1,250 injuries and the deaths of nineteen firefighters.

Safety concerns once led to a flirtation with alternatives to fire-engine red. The movement was fueled by research suggesting that hues of yellow or lime are more visible to the human eye, particularly at dusk or nighttime since they are more reflective. Indeed, support for a switch to yellow, lime green, or white from red was strong in the 1970s and 1980s. But subsequent analysis revealed little difference in the number of collisions.

It turns out that color has virtually no effect on how visible a fire truck is to motorists, but lighting and reflective surfaces do. The NFPA never had a requirement for fire truck color, but in 1991 it established new standards that increased the number and size of emergency lights and specified their brightness and location. It also added standards for the size, placement, and color of reflective striping. Though the Federal Aviation Administration stuck with lime-yellow for airport emergency vehicles, municipal fire departments have trended back to red. (Contrasting black or white upper bodies are considered chic for the best-dressed trucks.) The government's Occupational Safety and Health Administration also favors red in its standards.

Most firefighters couldn't be happier. They say that the public never really associated lime with fire trucks, and anything other than red somehow bucked a proud tradition. Any kid with a crayon in his hand could have told you as much.

Q Why do we trick or treat?

A   When you stop to think about it, trick-or-treating is a bit strange. We dress as a vampire, a princess, or a member of the opposite sex, then traipse from house to house, ringing doorbells and demanding treats. Most of the year, you'd get arrested for that kind of behavior. (Trust us.) But on Halloween, you're rewarded with candy.

Most historians agree that Halloween is derived from the ancient Celtic festival Samhain, which is held annually on November 1 to mark the end of the harvest season. The Celts believed that on the night before the festival, spirits of the dead were set free in the world of the living. To protect themselves, the Celts performed various rituals, such as building large bonfires. They also wore scary costumes—a precursor, some folklorists suggest, to our modern-day tradition of dressing up for Halloween.

Though humans have played dress-up for thousands of years, it was the British and Irish who struck upon the particular genius of donning a costume and then demanding gifts. From medieval times to well into the twentieth century, British islanders participated in the holiday tradition of "mumming"—prancing through the neighborhood in costume and asking for food and drink in exchange for a performance of a short play or song.

In Northern Ireland, in particular, this tradition continues with "Halloween rhyming," in which costumed children go door-to-door singing songs and hoping for a few pennies in return. During the massive Irish immigration to the United States in the late nineteenth and early twentieth centuries, immigrants brought along their Halloween traditions, including costumes.

Folklorists and historians are uncertain how a pleasant exchange of entertainment for pennies turned into the thinly disguised extortion of the American version. It appears the American custom of trick-or-treating didn't fully take hold until well into the twentieth century. The *Oxford English Dictionary* found the first use of the phrase "trick or treat" in print in 1947. That's not to say trick-or-treating was instantly accepted. In October 1954, a grumpy *Baltimore Sun* newspaper writer implored, "Now that the 'Trick-or-Treat' season is upon us, let us hope that thoughtful parents will discourage the practice."

It goes without saying that thoughtful parents did nothing of the sort. We have the Tootsie Rolls to prove it.

Q What is Sadie Hawkins Day?

A Sadie Hawkins Day sprang from the mind of cartoonist Al Capp and took on a life of its own. In the process, dating became a whole lot more entertaining.

On November 15, 1937, Sadie Hawkins Day was introduced to the fictional hillbilly town of Dogpatch, USA, in Capp's popular comic strip *Li'l Abner*. In the comic, Sadie Hawkins is "the homeliest gal in the hills." Frustrated by Sadie's inability to attract a suitor, her father, Hekzebiah Hawkins, seeks to upend traditional courting rituals by creating a footrace in which the town's unmarried women chase the available bachelors. If a man is caught by a woman, he has to marry her.

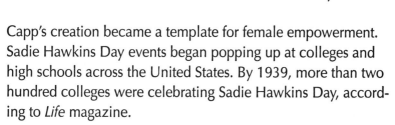

Capp's creation became a template for female empowerment. Sadie Hawkins Day events began popping up at colleges and high schools across the United States. By 1939, more than two hundred colleges were celebrating Sadie Hawkins Day, according to *Life* magazine.

Of course, the real-life version wasn't exactly like the one that was presented in the comic strip. There wasn't a frantic footrace that was followed by nuptials: Instead, women asked men for a date or to a dance featuring other Sadie Hawkins Day couples. In an era when women were subservient to men, it was a bold reversal of roles.

In Capp's comic, the race was run in November each year for several more decades. All the while, the popularity of Sadie Hawkins Day increased in the real world. *Li'l Abner* was discontinued in 1977, but Sadie Hawkins Day lives on, generally in the form of turnabout dances that take place in November. It remains a unique opportunity for an emboldened girl to make a play for an unsuspecting boy.

Q Why is Christmas on December 25?

A Is December 25 the day Jesus was born? Not likely. The Bible makes no mention of the birthdate of Jesus. And for the first two centuries of Christianity, observing the birthdays of martyrs was strongly discouraged—in part because celebrating birthdays was a pagan custom.

In its early years, the Roman Catholic Church gave little consideration to the precise day on which Jesus was born. Early in the fourth century, however, it apparently discovered a motivation to fix the date. According to the most popular and plausible explanation, the Roman Catholic Church chose December 25 in order to trump competing traditions.

Many dates for the birth had been proposed over the years. In AD 221, historian Sextus Julius Africanus wrote a lengthy world history that included Christianity and calculated December 25 as the day Jesus was born. The Roman Catholic Church found that this date suited its purposes, since December 25 was already set aside for pagan festivals that were popular among Romans. Among these were *natalis solis invicti* ("day of the birth of the unconquered sun") and the birthday of Mithra, or Mithras, a solar god also known as the Iranian god of light, who was worshipped by many Roman soldiers.

Generally, it's acknowledged that AD 336 was the year that the Roman Catholic Church established December 25 as the date of Jesus's birth. If the goal was to supplant pagan holidays with a Christian one, the decision clearly was a smashing success. As any Yule-season shopper can attest, it's really hard to find a "Merry Mithras" card these days.

Q How did Groundhog Day get started?

A It wasn't the brainchild of Punxsutawney Phil, the world's most famous weather-predicting groundhog. February 2, the day we observe as Groundhog Day, is important in the seasonal cycle. It falls halfway between the winter solstice—the shortest day of the year in the Northern Hemisphere—and the spring equinox, which is one of two days of equal sunlight and darkness.

This midpoint between winter and spring brings anticipation of a weather change from harsh cold to pleasant warmth. If we humans have an opportunity to believe that warm weather may come sooner rather than later, we'll take it. So weather-predicting became tied to this day.

The ancient Celts marked this halfway point with a holiday called Imbolc. Early Christians, meanwhile, routinely scheduled holidays to compete with and replace pagan holidays. February 2 is forty days after December 25, so Imbolc became Candlemas Day, an observance of the day Mary and Joseph took Jesus to the temple to perform the redemption of the firstborn. It was celebrated as a sort of end to the Christmas season.

The weather-predicting aspect of Candlemas Day carried over from pagan traditions. Europeans would place a candle in their windows on the eve of Candlemas Day. If the sun was out the next morning, they believed it indicated that there would be six more weeks of winter.

The predicting tools varied across Europe; in some places, they involved animals, such as bears, badgers, and, in Germany, the hedgehog. But requirements were the same: If it was sunny and the animal cast a shadow, it meant a longer winter; if it was cloudy and there was no shadow, it meant a shorter winter. When the hedgehog-watching Germans came to hedgehog-free America, they became groundhog-watching Americans. The earliest reference to Groundhog Day in America can be found in an 1841 diary by James Morris, a Pennsylvania shop owner.

With such a proud legacy, groundhogs can be counted on to be correct most of the time, right? Think again. A Canadian study showed that groundhogs are correct in predicting the length of winter only about 37 percent of the time.

Q Why do pawnshops display three balls outside?

A Pawnbrokers have been around for thousands of years—they plied their trade in ancient Greece, Rome, and China. Since the dawn of civilization, it seems, desperate men and women have had a place to go when they need fast cash, a place where they could put that chariot wheel in hock.

Even in today world, pawnbrokers maintain a healthy respect for tradition that befits the ancient beginnings of their noble trade. This nod to the past is probably best exemplified by the three balls that can be seen outside of many of the pawnshops around the globe. The origin of this three-ball design is shrouded in mystery, but we do know with some degree of certainty that it goes back hundreds of years—most likely to the Lombards of pre-Renaissance Europe.

The Lombard bankers—who hailed from Lombardy, a region on the northern end of the Italian peninsula in the foothills of the Alps—were essentially pawnbrokers, and it seems likely that they introduced the golden balls as their trademark wherever they opened shop. There are a number of theories about what the golden balls meant to the Lombard bankers.

Some people believe that they originally depicted three flat, gold circles, representing gold coins. It's possible that to attract more attention, the Lombards eventually changed their design to three-dimensional balls, each suspended separately from the same branch. Another theory suggests that the balls are derived from the golden pills that appear on the crest of the famous Medici family of northern Italy.

As the Lombards established pawnshops throughout Europe, the three balls became the general symbol of the trade. From mainland Europe, the symbol traveled to England, and early settlers in North America brought it with them. While these balls are no longer the universal emblem for pawnshops, they still can be spotted frequently.

So next time you're in a pawnshop, see if the proprietor knows why three yellow balls are hanging outside. If you enlighten him, maybe he'll give you a good deal.

Chapter Eight

EARTH AND SPACE

Q Are farmer's almanacs more accurate than the local weatherman?

A Well, they are more accurate when it comes to reporting blue-ribbon casserole recipes or amazing fishing stories. As for predicting the weather? Not so much.

The two leading farmer's almanacs are *Farmers' Almanac,* sold every year since 1818, and *The Old Farmer's Almanac,* sold every year since 1792. Both publish long-range weather predictions that they create using secret formulas, supposedly based in part on sunspot activity. And both claim to be 80 percent accurate or better. The problem is that the predictions are vague enough that assessing their accuracy is difficult.

For example, *The Old Farmer's Almanac*'s regional forecasts provide average temperatures and precipitation amounts for each month, with simple, impressionistic descriptions (e.g., "sunny, comfortable") for three- to seven-day blocks. So if it rains on one day in a seven-day block, should a "sunny" prediction be considered accurate?

It's not as hard as you might think for the almanac writers to hit the mark—they can do well just by looking at historical averages. For example, they can say with some authority that December in Minnesota will be cold and icy, and they can probably even guess an average temperature within five or ten degrees. Historical trends, then, are certainly a big part of their secret formulas.

Independent analyses suggest that the specific predictions in the almanacs are accurate a little more than half of the time, at best. For example, in 2004, meteorologist Nick Bond compared thirteen years of verifiable predictions from *The Old Farmer's* Almanac to the meteorological record. He concluded that the almanac was accurate about 50 percent of the time, which put it on par with random guessing.

How does that stack up against the forecast on your local news? Believe it or not, your weatherman's seven-day forecast might not be much more accurate than the almanac's. But one- to three-day forecasts are significantly more reliable, according to ForecastAdvisor.com, a Web site that tracks predictions from the major forecasting services. A sampling of its accuracy rankings shows that yearly scores typically fall between 70 and 85 percent, depending on the city. And these are fairly strict assessments of specific, daily predictions for precipitation and high and low temperatures, information that is more detailed than what the almanacs provide.

Then again, you can't take the local weatherman with you to the can. Every copy of *The Old Farmer's Almanac* has a hole in the upper left corner so that you can hang it on an outhouse nail. Try doing that with weather.com!

Q Is global warming causing more hurricanes?

A For the sake of answering this question, we'll presume the existence of global warming. (Among the general public, and even among those in the scientific community, a heated debate exists over whether humans are harming the atmosphere with our carbon dioxide pollution.) So, assuming global warming is in effect, what sorts of changes can we expect in the weather? Specifically, do the rising temperatures cause more hurricanes?

A 2007 release issued by the Intergovernmental Panel on Climate Change (IPCC) stated that while there has been an increase in hurricanes since 1995, a clear pattern has yet to emerge. The yearly hurricane average did not change much throughout most of the twentieth century—in North America, there were about five hurricanes a year; for the years between 1997 and 2006, the annual average was eight. There are scientists who are prepared to pin the increase on global warming; others think those scientists are crying wolf.

At the very least, it can be said with a degree of certainty that higher global temperatures create more hospitable conditions for hurricanes. In order for a hurricane to form, ocean waters must be at least eighty degrees Fahrenheit. When this temperature is reached, the atmosphere above the water becomes unstable—a fertile situation for tropical storms. It stands to reason that if Earth experiences an overall increase in temperature, ocean waters will reach this temperature more often. That's the speculation, anyway.

A less controversial topic involves hurricane intensity, which the IPCC says has probably worsened as a result of human activity. "More likely than not," the panel says—though these aren't the most definitive words ever spoken. The IPCC report predicts an increase in wind speeds and overall destructive capacities of hurricanes.

What can we glean from this information? There may or may not be more hurricanes because of increased levels of carbon dioxide in the atmosphere, but the eight or so we do get every year will knock our socks off.

Q If the moon causes tides, why does high tide happen twice a day?

A We've all been taught that the moon causes tides because of its gravitational pull. This is somewhat accurate, but our teachers weren't telling us the whole truth.

Let's start simply and then add the more complicated bits. The moon revolves around Earth, right? Wrong: Earth and the moon revolve around each other. More specifically, they revolve around a specific point, called the barycentre, where the moon and Earth balance each other out. This point is inside Earth, but it's closer to the surface than the core.

So Earth and the moon revolve around this point. Got it so far? Good. The moon exerts more pull on the side of Earth to which it's closest, which explains why you get a true high tide on only one side of the planet at a time. The moon pulls the ocean so that the water bulges a bit, and the nearby surfers are in for some sweet waves.

Because Earth is spinning around this barycentre, it is affected by a centrifugal force that points away from the moon. (Actually, "centrifugal force" in this case is something of a misnomer. Scientists like to talk about "rotating reference frames" and other silliness, but if you substitute the term "centrifugal force," it offers basically the same result and is simpler to understand. Scientists seem to be fond of making things as complicated as possible.) The moon exerts less gravitational pull on the far side of Earth, and centrifugal force takes charge, creating another bulge there. Two bulges at opposite ends mean two high tides a day.

So that about wraps up this question, neatly and tide-ily. (Sorry.)

Q What would happen if Earth stopped spinning?

A You know when you slam on the brakes in your car and the CDs and soda cans go flying? Now imagine slamming on the brakes when you're going 1,100 miles per hour, the planet's rotational speed at the equator. The instant that Earth stopped spinning, its atmosphere and inhabitants—along with soil, plants, buildings, oceans, and everything else that isn't firmly attached to the rocky foundation of the planet's crust—would keep on going at 1,100 miles per hour. The face of the planet would be wiped clean.

Let's say you were up in the Space Shuttle and missed all the planet-wiping excitement. What would life be like when you got back to now-still Earth? The good news is that there would be no change in gravity, which means that you wouldn't fall off the planet and the atmosphere wouldn't go away. But you would notice plenty of other differences. First of all, the cycles of day and night as we know them would no longer exist. Wherever you were, it would be light for about six months and then dark for about six months. As a result, one side of the planet would be icy cold and the other side would be extremely hot.

The planet's overall wind patterns would change significantly, too. Major wind patterns are caused by the sun heating the planet unevenly. The sun's rays hit the equator directly and the North Pole and South Pole at an angle, which means that the area around the equator gets much hotter than the mass around the poles. This heat gradient continually drives warmer air toward the poles and cooler air toward the equator, which establishes a basic global wind pattern.

But the spinning motion of the planet complicates this basic northerly and southerly airflow, creating smaller wind systems called convection cells in each hemisphere and leading to prevailing easterly and westerly winds. These systems interact to generate the weather that dictates the climate around the globe. If Earth didn't spin, we wouldn't see the same complex weather patterns. Warm air would simply rise at the equator and rush to the poles, and cold winds would move the opposite way.

Finally, a non-spinning Earth would stop generating a magnetic field. Yes, compasses would be useless, but there would be a much bigger problem: Earth would no longer possess the magnetic field's protection against cosmic rays. The radiation from the sun and other stars would damage your DNA, leading to severe health problems like cancer. But the extreme heat or cold and total lack of animal and plant life would kill you well before the nasty radiation kicked in.

Don't fret, though. There is virtually no chance that any of this could happen. For Earth's rotational speed to change radically, it would need to collide with an asteroid the likes of which we've never seen. Even if that happened, it's extremely unlikely that the collision would stop the planet from spinning altogether—it would probably just slow it down. In any case, we would see something that big well in advance, which would give Bruce Willis enough time to go and blow it up.

Q What happens to all the stuff we launch into space and don't bring back?

A Space trash creates a major traffic hazard. If you think it's nerve-wracking when you have to swerve around a huge pothole as you cruise down the highway, just imagine how it would feel if you were hundreds of miles above the surface of Earth, where the stakes couldn't be higher. That's the situation that the crew of the International Space Station (ISS) faced in 2008 when it had to perform evasive maneuvers to avoid debris from a Russian satellite.

And that was just one piece of orbital trash—all in all, there are tens of millions of junky objects that are larger than a millimeter and are in orbit. If you don't find this worrisome, imagine the little buggers zipping along at up to seventeen thousand miles per hour. Worse, these bits of flotsam and jetsam constantly crash into each other and shatter into even more pieces.

The junk largely comes from satellites that explode or disintegrate; it also includes the upper stages of launch vehicles, burnt-out rocket casings, old payloads and experiments, bolts, wire clusters, slag and dust from solid rocket mo-

tors, batteries, droplets of leftover fuel and high-pressure fluids, and even a space suit. (No, there wasn't an astronaut who came home naked—the suit was packed with batteries and sensors and was set adrift in 2006 so that scientists could find out how quickly a spacesuit deteriorates in the intense conditions of space.)

So who's responsible for all this orbiting garbage? The two biggest offenders are Russia—including the former Soviet Union—and the United States. Other litterers include China, France, Japan, India, Portugal, Egypt, and Chile. Each of the last three countries has launched one satellite during the past twenty years.

Most of the junk orbits Earth at between 525 and 930 miles from the surface. The Space Shuttle and the ISS operate a little closer to

Earth—the Shuttle flies at between 250 and 375 miles up, and the ISS maintains an altitude of about 250 miles—so they don't see the worst of it. Still, the ISS's emergency maneuver in 2008 was a sign that the situation is getting worse. Houston, we have a problem.

NASA and other agencies use radar to track the junk and are studying ways to get rid of it for good. Ideas such as shooting at objects with lasers or attaching tethers to some pieces to force them back to Earth have been discarded because of cost considerations and the potential danger to people on the ground. Until an answer is found, NASA practices constant vigilance, monitoring the junk and watching for collisions with working satellites and vehicles as they careen through space. Hazardous driving conditions, it seems, extend well beyond Earth's atmosphere.

Q Why do we give names to hurricanes and cyclones?

A Every year, as summer fades to fall, the news reports start: Teddy is wreaking havoc in the Caribbean; Bertha is causing trouble on the Eastern seaboard. We conjure images of shrill-voiced vacationers in straw hats, noses thick with sun block, making life miserable for restaurant servers and hotel clerks. But while Teddy and Bertha may sound like a nasty couple, they are, in fact, tropical storms.

Beyond anthropomorphizing storms, naming them has a practical application. There may be several storms brewing in the same region of the world at once. At one time, these storms were identified by their latitudinal and longitudinal coordinates. But that was clumsy and could result in miscommunication between forecasters and the public. Assigning storms short, distinct names is more effective.

The custom of naming storms has a long history. In the nineteenth century, hurricanes in the West Indies were named for the saint's day on which they arrived. During World War II, American armed forces meteorologists gave storms women's names, reportedly using the monikers of their wives and girlfriends for inspiration.

In 1953, after a brief period during which storm names were drawn from the phonetic alphabet (Able, Baker, Charlie, and so forth), U.S. forecasters revived the World War II custom of using women's names. The World Meteorological Organization has since assumed the coordination of the process in order to ensure international consistency. In the spirit of gender equality, the list of storm names began to alternate between male and female in 1979.

Today, tropical storms are named using rotating six-year lists. Each part of the world that is prone to tropical storms is assigned its own set of lists. The naming is done alphabetically: The year's first storm begins with A, the second with B, and so forth. The name of a particularly deadly or damaging storm is retired from the list.

If by chance you're a Quentin, Ursula, Xavier, Yuri, or Zubin, and you desire meteorological immortality, you had best attain it by becoming a famous TV weather forecaster. Why? So few names begin with Q, U, X, Y, and Z that these letters are excluded from the storm list.

Q Why do Space Shuttle astronauts wear parachutes?

A NASA devised an escape system for Space Shuttle missions after the 1986 Challenger disaster, in which seven astronauts died when a rocket booster exploded shortly after liftoff. The parachutes that astronauts now wear are part of a coordinated plan that offers them a chance to bail out if problems arise during launch or landing.

For obvious reasons, jumping from the shuttle is impossible while its rockets are firing. But there are scenarios in which escape would be an option. One would be after the rockets finish firing but before the shuttle reaches space. Another would be if the rockets fail after launch and the astronauts face a dangerous emergency landing in the ocean.

How would an escape work? First, the crew would guide the shuttle to an altitude of about twenty-five thousand to thirty thousand feet—just lower than the altitude reached by commercial airline flights—and jump from the craft through a side hatch.

To avoid hitting a wing or an engine pod during their escape, the astronauts would extend a twelve-foot pole from the side of the shuttle, hook themselves to it, slide down, and jump from there. NASA's space suits are designed to work automatically during an escape. The parachute opens at fourteen thousand feet, and when the suit detects impact with water, the parachute detaches.

The astronauts have other gizmos up their sleeves (and pant legs) that help in an emergency. When water is detected, the suit automatically deploys a life preserver. Also contained within the suit is a life raft, complete with a bailing cup to remove water that sloshes into it. Once safely afloat, the astronaut can pull a set of flares from one leg pocket and an emergency radio from the other. The suit, which is designed to keep the astronaut alive for twenty-four hours, is pressurized, thermal, and even comes equipped with a supply of drinking water.

The explosion that killed the Challenger crew was sudden and caused instant death, so this escape system would not have helped them. But because of that tragedy, today's Space Shuttle astronauts are better prepared if they need to make a daring escape.

Q What is the difference between a plant and a weed?

A One man's weed is another man's salad. Indeed, the simplest definition of a weed is a plant you don't like that's in the midst of plants you do like.

Take good old ground ivy. In your yard's natural area, it's a lovely ground cover; in your garden, it's a strangling weed. Dandelions, meanwhile, can be used for medicinal purposes, and they're edible-a little bacon, sliced hardboiled egg, chopped onion, and a dash of vinegar, and, mmm, you have a salad. On American lawns, however, dandelions are almost universally considered a hated weed.

A weed is a nuisance in a lawn or garden because it competes for sun, water, and nutrients with the plants that you desire. Weeds are hardy and maddeningly adaptable. They can be annuals, like crabgrass, which produces seeds for one season; they'll drive you nuts and then die off. Or they can be biennials, which bloom and then go dormant for two years. The classy sounding Queen Anne's lace, also known as the wild carrot, is a biennial weed.

Perennial weeds are the guests that won't leave. They hunker down and mooch off the "good" plants. They're often buggers to get rid of. Dandelions are classic perennials and have a highly effective seed-spreading system—every time a breeze or a kid blows the white puffy seeds off a dandelion, hundreds of opportunities for new dandelion plants fly through the air.

If you've decided that the thing growing in your yard is a weed and not a plant, how do you kill it? You can douse it with herbicides (be careful not to hurt the "good plants") or smother it with newspaper, plastic, or landscaping cloth. Or you can yank it from the ground, but remember that many weeds are very resilient, and if a morsel of root is left behind, it'll return again and again, like *Rocky* movies.

The alternative is to simply relax, fry up some bacon, dice an onion, and get out the salad bowls.

Q Can you go blind looking at a solar eclipse?

A This one seems to have B.S. written all over it. In grade school, you were warned about looking at a solar eclipse, but if this danger were real, wouldn't there be blind people everywhere? Consider: It's the day of the eclipse, the sky starts to darken, you look up to see what's going on, and boom—you're poking your way around with a white cane for the rest of your life. Where's the logic? Well, amazingly, the concept here isn't a complete load.

First off, staring at the sun at any time isn't a good idea. Prolonged exposure to the ultraviolet radiation from the sun can damage the nerve endings in the eye, leading to vision problems such as spotting, blurriness, and, in extreme cases, blindness. Exposing the retina to intense visible light causes damage to its light-sensitive rod and cone cells.

The light can trigger a series of complex chemical reactions within the cells that damages their ability to respond to a visual stimulus and, in extreme cases, can destroy them. There are many factors that affect how your eyes will respond to this kind of abuse, including the size and color of your eyes, preexisting eye problems, and the angle of the sun.

As a result, it is difficult to say exactly how long one can look at the sun without injury, but you should try to limit your exposure to less than a minute. While this might not seem like much time, think about how difficult and painful it is to keep your eyes trained on the sun for even ten seconds. What makes solar eclipses so dangerous is that the stare-prohibiting glare of the sun is greatly diminished.

Just how dangerous are eclipses? Staring at one won't cause instant blindness. Furthermore, the term "blindness" is a bit of an overstatement—eye impairments can be as minor as a slight discoloration in the visual field. This type of damage typically is temporary, and many people recover their normal vision within a few weeks.

So the warnings from your grade-school teachers were slightly exaggerated. Still, their general message was sound: It's never a bright idea to stare at that bright ball in the sky.

Q Why is the sky blue?

A What if the sky were some other color? Would a verdant green inspire the same placid happiness that a brilliant blue sky does? Would a pink sky be tedious for everyone except girls under the age of fifteen? What would poets and songwriters make of a sky that was an un-rhymable orange?

We'll never have to answer these questions, thanks to a serendipitous combination of factors: the nature of sunlight, the makeup of Earth's atmosphere, and the sensitivity of our eyes.

If you have seen sunlight pass through a prism, you know that light, which to the naked eye appears to be white, is actually made up of a rainbow-like spectrum of colors: red, orange, yellow, green, blue, and violet. Light energy travels in waves, and each of these colors has its own wavelength. The red end of the spectrum has the longest wavelength, and the violet end has the shortest.

The waves are scattered when they hit particles, and the size of the particles determines which waves get scattered most effectively. As it happens, the particles that make up the nitrogen and oxygen in the atmosphere scatter shorter wavelengths of light much more effectively than longer wavelengths. The violets and the blues in sunlight are scattered most prominently, and reds and oranges are scattered less prominently.

However, since violet waves are shorter than blue waves, it would seem that violet light would be more prolifically scattered by the atmosphere. So why isn't the sky violet? Because there are variations among colors that make up the spectrum of sunlight—there isn't as much violet as there is blue. And because our eyes are more sensitive to blue light than to violet light, blue is easier for our eyes to detect.

That's why, to us, the sky is blue. And we wouldn't want it any other way.

Chapter Nine

SPORTS

Q Which sport has the worst athletes?

A We know what you're thinking: bowling. It's an obvious choice, but you're wrong. We know what you've witnessed at your local bowling alley, and, yes, it's tragic. But comparing those people to pro bowlers, who need the physical and mental stamina to compete on far less forgiving lanes and bowl up to one hundred games a week, is like comparing those chunky, red-faced softball players at your local park to major-league baseball players.

And no, it's not baseball, either—John Kruk notwithstanding. (In response to a fan who chided him during his playing days for his less-than-exemplary physique, the corpulent Kruk replied, "I ain't an athlete, lady, I'm a baseball player.")

Golf is a common target for those who wish to identify nonathletes, and the sport has indeed featured some Krukian figures, such as the generously proportioned John Daly. Still, the strength and stamina it takes to get that darned ball from the tee to the hole—while walking about twenty to twenty-five miles over the course of a tournament—qualifies as athletic prowess. (You snicker, but when was the last time you walked twenty-five miles in a week?)

How about the luge? Now we're getting somewhere. Who among us hasn't spent an entire Sunday afternoon "practicing the luge" (i.e., prostrate on the couch in front of the TV, watching other people sweat)? Turns out, though, that real lugers have tremendous upper-body strength and spend their off-seasons lifting weights and swimming. Who knew?

So we turn to curling, which, as we are all aware, is basically just shuffleboard for aging Canadians who haven't yet broken their hips. At the 2006 Winter Olympics, United States curler Scott Baird competed at the age of fifty-four. And yet, there is agility involved—it's kind of like bowling on ice. And did you see that "women of curling" nude calendar that made a splash during those same 2006 Olympics? We defy you to tell us that those bodies weren't athletic.

Okay, time to get serious. Which sport has the worst athletes? We planned to choose darts, which requires participants to spend as much time as possible in bars, where breaking a sweat has more to do with the TV lighting than the action. But then we stumbled upon the Cyberathlete Professional League (CPL). That's right: professional video gamers posing as athletes.

Sure, this seems like a typical case of the jocks picking on the nerds. But the CPL (before it folded in 2008) went to great lengths to portray itself as a real, big-time sports league, right down to its red, white, and blue logo that mimicked the classic NBA and Major League Baseball logos—a silhouetted figure (seated, of course) wearing headphones and pumping one fist in the air exultantly while the other hand daintily fingers a mouse. In other words, they were asking for it. A sport of computer geeks. A sport with an "official pizza" (Pizza Hut). That's the sport with the worst athletes.

Q Why do you have to be quiet when a golfer is swinging?

A At first blush, the answer seems obvious: So the golfer can concentrate. But it brings up interesting subsequent questions: Why do golfers insist that they be allowed to concentrate when, say, football and baseball players do not? The answers have to do with the particular demands of golf and the particular social milieu in which it's been played for several centuries.

Let's start with the physical and mental demands. There is probably no other sport that requires such a combination of power and precision—of power applied precisely. Tiger Woods propels a full drive at about 150 miles per hour, yet he's envisioning a landing area that's not much more than ten yards wide, some 240 yards down the fairway.

If one part of Tiger's body moves more than a fraction of an inch in the wrong way while he swings, or if the timing of his swing is imprecise—he releases his wrists a fraction of a second too soon, say—the ball can travel thirty, forty, fifty yards or more off-target.

It's just as demanding on the green. Two hundred years ago, golf greens were as shaggy as a carpet. Now, the better the course, the shorter the greens are. At Augusta National Golf Club during the Masters Tournament, they are just a little more forgiving than linoleum. Tiger needs to control every nuance of the length, speed, and pace of his putting swing in order to prevent the ball from scurrying yards past the hole. This—like his drive—requires fantastic physical coordination, sensory sophistication, and concentration.

But not too much concentration. The hallmark of a hack golfer is his reliance on a mental checklist before every swing. "Head down, shoulder tucked, left arm straight..." Tiger has drilled these requisites into his unconscious mind—and into his muscles. But in order for that natural process to take place as programmed—in order to achieve the right combination of concentration and calm—he needs quiet. Tiger is so routinized, in fact, that he loses his temper when fans make unexpected noises or take pictures during his swing.

Maybe if golfers grew up amid bedlam, like football players do, they wouldn't mind the distractions. But they're accustomed to quiet. Which gets to the matter of tradition. For much of its history, golf has been a club sport. Clubs are laden with rules that seem arbitrary and stuffy to outsiders but make the social experience more meaningful for members. There are all sorts of formalities in golf clubs regarding gentlemanly behavior and the like, and these have extended to the course, where golfers go out of their way to observe them.

For example, the player who had the lowest score on the previous hole always tees off first on the next. If someone forgets and accidentally tees off out of turn, it's embarrassing, even among good friends. This powerful social component of golf colors every minute on the course, and keeping quiet during a golfer's swing is the most obligatory courtesy. So you see, as with almost everything in golf, there's more to this custom than meets the eyes ... and ears.

Q Why does K stand for strikeout?

A To the uninitiated, a baseball scorecard can look like hieroglyphs in need of the Rosetta stone: numbers, circles, lines, colored diamonds, and more abbreviations than an IM conversation between hyperactive teens. And when the seven-dollar beers start flowing in the grandstand—forget about it.

Actually, most of these abbreviations are fairly easy to decipher. It doesn't take a sabermetrician to figure out that HR stands for "home run" and BB stands for "base on balls." But what genius designated K the symbol for "strikeout"?

That would be Henry Chadwick—writer, National Baseball Hall of Fame member, and inventor of the baseball box score. Chadwick was born in England in 1824 and grew up as an avid fan ot the English ball games cricket and rounders. He emigrated to the

United States as a young man, and in the 1850s, as the relatively new sport of baseball gained popularity in America, Chadwick became a devoted fan. Chadwick was a newspaper reporter in New York at the time, and at his urging, the city's major newspapers added coverage of baseball games to their agendas.

A lot happens in a baseball game, and Chadwick knew that it wasn't always easy to keep track of what was going on—especially when the thirteen-cent beers started flowing in the grandstand. In 1861, in a treatise curiously titled *Beadle's Dime Base-Ball Player*, Chadwick introduced a scorecard for baseball games. It was adapted from one used by reporters to keep track of cricket matches.

Chadwick's early scorecard was an unwieldy, Excel-worthy spreadsheet. It involved twenty-nine columns that were thirteen rows deep, and provided space for stats of the day like "bounds" and "muffs." It also included space to record what happened on a play-to-play basis, which helped writers recreate the game in the next day's newspaper.

Because S was so common in baseball's statistical lexicon ("stolen base," "sacrifice," "strikeout"), Chadwick chose K to represent the whiff. Why K? It's the last letter in "struck," which was the common term that was used to describe the strikeout in the 1860s.

The baseball scorecard has grown more comprehensible over the years, but much of Chadwick's original form and symbolism survives, including the use of K for a strikeout. Nowadays, many fans take it further by using a normal K to represent a swinging strikeout and a backward K to represent a called third strike.

Chadwick, who devoted his life to promoting baseball, would no doubt delight at the immense popularity the game has attained. It's doubtful that he'd be impressed by the beer sales, however: Chadwick was a strong supporter of the temperance movement.

Q Shouldn't the Los Angeles Lakers be called the Oceaners instead?

A They probably should be, given the team's proximity to the Pacific Ocean and the conspicuous lack of lakes in the Los Angeles area. But it's not that simple. For those of you who don't know anything about the history of the National Basketball Association (NBA) before Michael Jordan, here's a lesson. The Lakers didn't originate in Los Angeles—they came from Minneapolis, where they were, in the 1950s, the NBA's first dynasty.

Actually, the team that became the Lakers started in Detroit, as the Gems of the National Basketball League (NBL), a predecessor of the NBA. Ben Berger and Morris Chalfen purchased the franchise in 1944 and moved it to Minneapolis three years later. They renamed the team "Lakers," an acknowledgement of Minnesota's status as the "Land of 10,000 Lakes."

Since the Gems were the worst team in the NBL in the 1946–47 season, the Lakers got the first pick in a dispersal draft of players from the defunct Professional Basketball League of America, which earned them the rights to George Mikan, the first "greatest" player in pro basketball history. With Mikan, the Lakers won the

NBL title in 1948; jumped to the Basketball Association of America and won its title in 1949; then joined the newly formed NBA and won titles in 1950, 1952, 1953, and 1954. But the booming Los Angeles market was too tempting to resist—especially considering that attendance dropped significantly in Minneapolis after Mikan retired following the 1953–54 season—and the Lakers became the NBA's first West Coast franchise in 1960.

As for the matter at hand: No, it doesn't make sense to call a Los Angeles team the Lakers. The only lake of significance around the city is north of the downtown area, at Echo Park. But we're not going to pick on L.A.'s basketball team for being associated with a lake instead of an ocean. At least not until the NBA's Utah Jazz return their incongruous and ludicrous nickname to the city where they originated, New Orleans, and adopt something more area-appropriate—like the Slalom, the Flats, or the Mormons.

Q Why are there stripes on bowling pins?

A As any modern-day hipster can tell you, bowling is more about fashion than rolling a ball into a rack of pins. So perhaps it's not surprising that even bowling pins pay homage to the style gods. With a pair of sweet stripes like an ascot around its neck, a bowling pin resembles a 1950s Frenchman on a yacht trip off the Riviera.

Okay, so maybe bowling pins aren't inspired by haute couture. (But don't try to tell us those shoes aren't!) Actually, bowling pins are a classic case of form following function. It's been a long evolution: Archaeologists have found evidence of bowling pins dating back almost two thousand years.

Those first bowling pins were made of stone, but by the late nineteenth century, bowling-pin manufacturers had turned to maple as their material of choice. These early pins were made from a solid block of wood, but problems with splintering and uneven weights led to inconsistent pin behavior and lower scores than bowling's governing body at the time, the American Bowling Congress (ABC), liked to see.

Pin manufacturers eventually discovered that gluing pieces of maple wood together and coating them with a synthetic lacquer not only made it easier to produce pins with more consistent weights, but also resulted in a sturdier pin. Pins are still generally made from maple, despite experiments with steel, plastic, and even magnesium.

Nowadays, all bowling pins are standardized according to specifications set by the United States Bowling Congress (or USBC, as the former ABC is now known). These specifications include height and weight measurements, as well as the circumference of different parts of the pin. Nowhere in the specs, however, is there a mention of stripes, though the USBC does allow for pins to have "neck markings."

So why stripes? According to representatives of both the USBC and Brunswick Bowling, there is no particular reason. The striping convention first appeared early in the twentieth century, as bowling's popularity grew and companies began mass-producing bowling equipment. These stripes were nothing more than a form of decoration—a stylistic flourish.

Stripes aren't the only bits of flair to appear on pin necks. For example, Brunswick manufacturers some pins with crowns around the necks. We, however, are partial to the image of ten Frenchmen in ascots. It's way more fashionable.

Q Why is there a dropped-third-strike rule in baseball?

A On the surface, baseball is pretty simple. In the memorable words of former major-league manager Lee Elia: "The name of the game is hit the ball, catch the ball, and get the [bleeping] job done." But getting the [bleeping] job done and maintaining that apparent simplicity requires a few rules for resolving unusual situations—for example, the infield fly and the balk—that most fans know about without ever fully understanding.

Such is the case with the dropped-third-strike rule (or, more accurately, the uncaught-third-strike rule). The philosophy behind the rule is based on common sense: A team in the field shouldn't be given credit for an out if it screws up at the end of the play. On a third strike, if the catcher drops the pitch, or if the pitch bounds away from the catcher, it's equivalent to any other fielder dropping a fly ball. The batter is free to try to reach first base, and the defense has to be more proactive to record the out, by either tagging the batter or throwing him out at first base.

Without some modifications, the dropped-third-strike rule would offer the defense an unfair advantage. This is where the rule gets a little confusing. Say there's a runner on first and no outs—on a third strike, the catcher could purposely drop the ball, obliging the batter to run to first, which would in turn oblige the runner on first to make a break for second. With the batter and runner caught off-guard, the catcher could pick up the ball and initiate an easy double play by throwing to second for the force-out, followed by a quick throw from second to first to retire the now-running batter.

To eliminate the possibility of this sort of chicanery, the dropped-third-strike rule only applies under the following conditions: when there are two outs and a double play is pointless, or when first base is open with fewer than two outs so there is no chance for a force-out. With fewer than two outs and first base occupied, the batter is out on strike three regardless of whether the catcher catches the pitch.

The infield fly rule is also designed to eliminate similarly cheap double (or triple) plays initiated by intentional errors with runners on base. Now, if you want to figure out the [bleeping] balk rule, you'll have to go to another [bleeping] article.

Q Why would you want to put "English" on the cue ball?

A Pool is a game with a long history. Also known as pocket billiards (which distinguishes it from carom billiards, snooker, and other billiard games that are played on pocketless tables), pool was once seen in a negative light because it was associated with seediness, drinking, and gambling. (In short, trouble—right here in River City.) Although it's still popular to play pool in bars—and to bet on the outcome—pool tables have migrated toward respectability, becoming staples of rec centers and family basements.

Pool seems fairly simple at first glance, whether you're playing eight-ball, nine-ball, or any of the game's countless other variations. Of course, you need some basic skills—for a beginner, for example, it might be difficult to even hit the cue ball without ripping up the felt. But once you've got the basics down, you'll notice that the simple rules of geometry govern the motion of the pool balls when they bounce off of each other or the side rail. Knowledge of these rules allows a competent player to predict the exact route that the ball will take.

And this is where "English" comes in. Putting English on the ball is a way to momentarily suspend the laws of geometry and to change the predicted outcome when the cue ball hits the rail or another ball. It's done by striking the cue stick slightly off-center—the ball still travels in a straight line, but it has spin on it, which changes the effect of its impact.

If you put left or right English on the ball, it changes the angle that it takes when it bounces off the rail—and it changes the angle that the other balls take when they get hit. You can also give a ball "follow" or "draw." If you put follow on the cue ball, the topspin will cause it to follow after the ball that it hits; if you use draw on the cue ball, the spin will bring it back toward you after it hits its target. There's also "stop," which makes the cue ball freeze after it bangs into another ball.

Why is it called English? It's only called that in the United States; cue-ball spin is known as "side" in England, where the technique was invented. English manufacturers started adding tips to cues in the early eighteen hundreds. Not only did the tip enable the player to make better contact with the cue ball, but it also allowed for deflection. English pool players who visited the United States demonstrated their mastery by making seemingly impossible shots—and inspiring their slack-jawed American opponents to call the technique "English."

If you want to improve your pool game, learning how to put English on the cue ball is one way to do it. But the cat's out of the bag—unlike when those British pool sharks visited America, everyone now knows about English, so don't expect to impress anyone with your technique.

Q Why do marathon runners wrap themselves in foil after a race?

A Watching thousands of marathon runners clog the streets of a major city is odd. Odder still is the sight of these runners huddled in foil wrappers after the race. What are those things anyway?

After suffering through 26.2 miles of agony on the pavement, it seems that the last thing you would need is someone packaging you up like you're about to be sold off of a downtown food cart. But in fact, you cover a runner in foil for the same reason you would a baked potato or a burrito—to keep in heat.

These foil coverings are called HeatSheets, and they can be life-savers for people who run marathons, particularly in cold weather. Runners shed clothing as they move through a long-distance race, usually finishing in shorts and a T-shirt. The body heats up during a race and, therefore, sweats as a cooling mechanism. It's virtually impossible for a runner to drink enough liquid during a race to offset the moisture he or she loses through sweating, so dehydration sets in. This also prevents the body from cooling properly.

That's not a huge problem until the end of the race, when a runner begins to cool down—rapidly, if the weather is chilly. The cool-down can happen so quickly that it fools the body's internal sensors, which haven't gotten the message that the race is over and continue to shed heat. In such a case, dehydration quickly turns to hypothermia.

HeatSheets prevent the rapid loss of body heat. They're made of Mylar (a plastic sheeting) and coated with a thin layer of aluminum, which keeps heat trapped against the body. In addition, because of their economical size, HeatSheets are better to hand out after a race than, say, blankets or sweatshirts. They just look a lot sillier.

Q What's the farthest anyone has hit a baseball?

A There isn't a reliable answer, and here's why: While everything within the confines of the field of play in professional baseball—including the dimensions of those confines—is scrupulously measured and recorded, the stuff outside the field of play is up for grabs.

There are numerous falsehoods regarding the farthest anyone has hit a baseball. For years, *Guinness World Records* has stated that Mickey Mantle of the New York Yankees hit a ball 565 feet at Griffith Stadium in Washington, D.C., on April 17, 1953, calling it "the longest measured home run." Well, it turns out that it was measured to the point where a neighborhood kid picked up the ball, not necessarily where it actually landed.

Other similarly gargantuan blows have come into question. Dave Nicholson of the Chicago White Sox hit one at Chicago's Comiskey Park on May 6, 1964, that team "mathematicians" pegged at 573 feet. But as historian William J. Jenkinson pointed out, the mathematicians based their calculation on the belief that the ball cleared the roof; in fact, it hit the back of the roof before escaping the stadium.

The *New York Times* reported that a blast by Dave Kingman of the New York Mets at Chicago's Wrigley Field on April 14, 1976, went 630 feet. The homer, which bounced off a building across the street, was later measured at 530 feet, though even that number is based on conjecture.

By now, you've probably noticed that there hasn't been much hard science applied to determining the longest ball ever hit; instead, it's been a mishmash of speculation. However, that is changing. Greg Rybarcyzk, creator of the Web site Hit Tracker, measures the distance of every home run hit by using a complex formula that includes time of flight, initial trajectory, atmospheric conditions, and so on. If his calculations are wrong, it's going to take a wise man with a lot of time on his hands to prove them so. Since Rybarcyzk's Hit Tracker began measuring homers in 2005, no one has hit a ball more than five hundred feet—the 490s is about as Herculean as a blast has gotten.

This somewhat supports the work of Robert Adair, a Yale physics professor who states in his book *The Physics of Baseball* that the farthest a human can possibly hit a baseball is 545 feet. Adair's claim calls into further dispute the dozens of anecdotal moon shots that are part of baseball lore, including Mantle's and Nicholson's. And while Adair's number doesn't answer the question, it at least puts us in the ballpark.

Chapter Ten

PLACES

Q Why are we supposed to remember the Alamo?

A The average three-year-old in Texas can probably tell you the tale of the Alamo, complete with names, dates, and cool sound effects. But it's understandable if the details are a little hazy for the rest of us. We have our own state histories to worry about.

The Alamo began as a Roman Catholic mission called Misión San Antonio de Valero, which was established by the Spanish in the early eighteenth century to convert Native Americans to Christianity. The missionaries moved out in 1793, and nine years later, a Spanish cavalry company moved in, turning it into a fort that it called the Alamo (after Alamo de Parras, the city in Mexico that had been the company's home base). When the Mexican War of Independence ended in 1821, Mexican soldiers had control of all of San Antonio, including the Alamo, and they built up the fort's defenses.

But no one cares if you remember any of this stuff. You're supposed to remember the Alamo because of what happened there during the Texas Revolution. This was a conflict between the Mexican government and the Texians-people who had moved to Mexican territory from the United States. The Texians chafed under the government of Mexican president General Antonio López de Santa Anna Pérez de Lebrón (or Santa Anna to his friends), who was trying to assert more central control over the region. The Texians rebelled against this crackdown and took control of San Antonio and the Alamo, among other places.

On February 23, 1836, General Santa Anna and thousands of soldiers showed up to reclaim the Alamo. William Travis, the commander of the Texian insurgents who held the Alamo, sent messengers out to request help from surrounding communities. He got only thirty-two more volunteers, bringing his fighting force up to about two hundred men. Though they were clearly outnumbered, Travis and his men decided that they would rather die than surrender the fort. They held out for thirteen days, but in a final assault on March 6, Santa Anna's soldiers took control of the fort and killed Travis and all of his men.

The defeat infuriated the Texian revolutionaries and strengthened their resolve. Two months later at the Battle of San Jacinto, Texian soldiers led by General Sam Houston shouted, "Remember the Alamo!" as they charged into the fray. The rebels defeated the Mexican army, captured Santa Anna, and won Texas its independence. "Remember the Alamo!" became a rallying cry, and the battle went down in history as a tale of brave men standing their ground against terrible odds.

The resulting Republic of Texas was short-lived and unstable, thanks in part to continued skirmishes with the Mexican army. On December 29, 1845, Texas became a U.S. state, and soon Mexico and the United States were embroiled in the Mexican-American War. But that's another story for another book. In the meantime, any Texas toddler should be able to tell you all about it.

Q Why do they drive on the left side of the road in England?

A Or if you're from England: Why do Americans drive on the right side of the road? At any rate, it probably goes back to the good old Romans, who, we're fairly certain, drove on the left. Bryn Walters, a British archaeologist, discovered a Roman track in England that led to an ancient quarry. On the left-hand side, running out of the quarry, the track was deeply grooved by wagon wheels; Walters surmised that this was because the wagons were laden with stone and, therefore, were heavier. How did he reach this conclusion? The other side of the road was less deeply worn, presumably because it was used by empty wagons that were going into the quarry to collect their loads.

Fast-forward to the Middle Ages, when you never knew who you were going to meet on the road (though you could be pretty sure that he'd be smelly). A popular "left side" theory is that people needed to be able to easily whip out their swords to defend themselves. Because most people were right-handed, they rode on the left to leave their sword arms free to whack foes.

Regardless of how things went down, the British rode on the left long before the "keep left" law was introduced in the seventeen hundreds. So why have so many other countries opted for the right? One explanation posits that when Napoleon started conquering countries in the early eighteen hundreds, he forced the vanquished to drive on the right, in defiance of the hated English. America, meanwhile, liked the thought of being revolutionary— and the idea of annoying the English—so it also went for the right.

According to another explanation, modes of transportation developed differently in different places. In the United States and France, a typical horse-drawn wagon had no driver's seat. Instead, the driver sat on the left-rear horse so that his right arm was free to wield a whip and persuade his good-for-nothing beasts to go faster. In order to communicate with other riders, the driver would ride on the right-hand side of the road so he was next to any oncoming traffic.

Britain's horse-drawn carts had driver's seats. Again, the driver would typically use his right hand to whip the horses. Since he didn't want the whip to get caught up in the load behind him as he swung, he sat on the right. Again, he needed to keep an eye on, and communicate with, oncoming traffic, so he drove on the left.

About two-thirds of the world's countries now drive on the right; among those still on the left are Britain, India, Australia, South Africa, and Japan. So if you're terrified of trying to drive a car on the left and you happen to be in one of those countries, a word of advice: Use public transportation.

Q Where is No Man's Land?

A For a place so desolate, No Man's Land sure has a lot of locations. Take a look at a map and you will find a No Man's Land in the Caradon district of southeast Cornwall, England; a No Man's Land on East Falkland Island; and a Nomans Land Island (also charted No Man's Land or No Man's Island) in Chilmark, Massachusetts. And that's just to name a few.

Some of these places are indeed uninhabited, but that's probably for good reason. In the case of the Falkland Island No Man's Land, the terrain is extremely rough due to a craggy chain of mountains known as Wickham Heights.

And the No Man's Land in Massachusetts? It is located only three miles off the quaint coast of Martha's Vineyard, but this island was once used as a practice range for bombing. It's closed to the public, apparently due to concern about unexploded ordnance that still might detonate.

In more general terms, No Man's Land is a phrase that has been around since at least the fourteenth century. It's often used to reference an unoccupied area between the front lines of opposing armies, or to designate land that is unowned, undesirable, or otherwise under dispute.

A good example: Following the Louisiana Purchase between the United States and Spain, an area called No Man's Land (a.k.a. the Neutral Strip or Sabine Free State) was designated neutral ground because the two governments could not agree on a boundary. From 1806 to 1819, both countries claimed ownership of this tract, but neither enforced any laws or control. No wonder it became a haven for outlaws and renegades.

In its earliest use, No Man's Land likely referred to a plot of land just outside the north walls of London. In the early thirteen hundreds, this No Man's Land was a place where criminals were executed and left out in the open for public view. There goes the neighborhood.

Q Why is Chicago called the Windy City?

A Chicago has its own special set of reputations. It's known for blue-collar workers, a losing baseball team, corrupt politicians, and heart attack-inducing foods. The city also has its share of nicknames, such as the Second City and the City of Big Shoulders. For most people, though, Chicago is the Windy City. But why?

Any shivering tourist visiting downtown Chicago during the winter could justifiably assume that this nickname is descriptive of the arctic gales that whip off Lake Michigan. Helpful Chicagoans are quick to rectify this apparent misconception. They explain that Chicago is the Windy City not for meteorological reasons, but because of its great tradition of windbag politicians. The exact phrase is said to date back to

1890, when New York and Chicago battled for the right to host the 1893 World's Fair. The bluster from Chicago politicians in support of their city's bid led Charles Dana, editor of *The* (New York) *Sun,* to urge his readers to reject "the nonsensical claims of that windy city."

For many years, this theory was accepted as fact. It was most recently rehashed by writer Erik Larson in his bestselling book about the 1893 World's Fair, *The Devil in the White City.* One minor hitch: There is no published record of such a statement attributed to Dana. According to Barry Popik, an etymologist who has tracked down the origins of many uniquely American nicknames and slang phrases, the nickname Windy City was introduced long before 1890. Popik says that the first recorded use of the nickname can be traced to 1860 and, perhaps not surprisingly, was indeed related to the strong winds that blow off the lake. In fact, according to Popik, Chicago promoted its windy reputation in an effort to sell itself as a resort destination. (Surely this was one of the least-enticing advertising campaigns in tourism history.)

Still, the theory that links the nickname to windbag politicians might have some credence. In the second half of the nineteenth century, Chicago and Cincinnati waged a fierce war of words over which of the two cities should be considered the pearl of the Midwest. (St. Louis wanted to get in on the rivalry, but it was, you know, St. Louis.) As huge numbers of Americans moved west, midwestern cities tried to lure new residents with advertising and braggadocio, a phenomenon known as boosterism.

Chicago and Cincinnati were major hog-slaughtering centers (apparently a big draw in the nineteenth century), and both boasted about their waterfront views. It didn't take long for Cincinnati newspapers to pick up on the double entendre of "windy" with regard to Chicago. Editorials in Cincinnati newspapers hammered away at Chicago's weather and the empty bluster of its booster-ism, successfully saddling their rival to the north with the Windy City moniker. At the same time, Cincinnati won a nickname that signified its meatpacking supremacy: Porkopolis. Who's having the last laugh now?

Q Why are the southern U.S. states called Dixie?

I wish I was in the land of cotton,
Old times there are not forgotten,
Look away, look away,
Look away, Dixieland.

A Where exactly is Dixieland? If you look on a map of the United States, you won't find it. Not a single state, major river, or mountain range is named Dixie. Yet everyone knows about the place. Ask any American and the answer will be that the South is Dixie. And if that person is a history buff, you'll be told that it's been that way since the Civil War. But why? Why is the South called Dixie?

There are several explanations. The most obvious refers to the Ma-son–Dixon Line, a border that was drawn in 1767 by two English surveyors, Charles Mason and Jeremiah Dixon, to settle a dispute between Pennsylvania and Maryland. After Pennsylvania abol-ished slavery in 1781, the Mason-Dixon Line became the de facto border between the free and slave states. The southern side, or

"Dixon's land," eventually morphed into "Dixieland." This makes sense. But you have to wonder why southerners would want to use the name of an Englishman who never lived among them.

Maybe we should try following the money. Follow it all the way down to New Orleans in the early eighteen hundreds, and you'll find ten-dollar bills printed with the French word *dix* ("ten," pronounced "deece") being paid to planters who sold their cotton in the market. (The Louisiana Creole favored French money, so the Citizens Bank of Louisiana printed money with American currency denominations on one side and French denominations on the other.) Ten dollars was a lot of money in those days, and planters who made a big sale would brag about the number of "dixies" they raked in. As they couldn't speak French, they came down hard on the x, and Dixie was born. Soon, any place where this highly desirable currency circulated became known as Dixieland.

Even so, the name might have faded into history if not for Ohio-born Yankee songwriter Dan Emmett. In 1859, he published a banjo ditty called "I Wish I Was in Dixie." The song became quite popular on the minstrel circuit. Though it was reportedly a big favorite of none other than Abraham Lincoln himself, southerners readily embraced it as their unofficial anthem during the Civil War.

Because of its connections with slavery and black-face minstrel shows, many people today feel that Dixieland music has racist connotations. Some historians, however, believe that Emmett got the song from two African American musicians, Ben and Lew Snowden, with whom he occasionally performed in Ohio. This makes Dixie part of the black as well as white tradition. Recently, a few jazz musicians have begun to explore this idea, mixing the tune with black gospel and blues. After all, if it was good enough for Abraham Lincoln, it should be good enough for the rest of us, too.

Q Why is Maine called "Down East"?

A The state of Maine occupies the northeastern-most corner of the United States. You might think, therefore, that when people in Boston, which is fifty miles to the south, take a jaunt to Maine, they would say they're going "up to Maine" for the summer and returning "down to Boston" when the season is over. Instead, Bostonians, or at least the old-fashioned "proper" ones, will tell you that they're going "down to Maine" and coming back "up to Boston." Say what? Have they lost their compass?

Not exactly. The phrase "down east" comes from sailors' lingo. Back in the nineteenth century, the fastest way to travel was by clipper ship. Fortunately, a steady wind from the south swept up the East Coast, pushing ships northeast. When sailors travel with the wind at their backs, they say they are traveling downwind. "Down east" means going east with the wind behind you. Returning south, ships would be pushing against the wind, or upwind.

Pretty simple. But in this day and age, when most vacationers arrive by interstate highway, why do Mainers still like to call their state Down East? Maybe it's because people who can stick it out in a land of long, dark winters are pretty darn proud of their history and like to celebrate it in all kinds of unique ways, from choosing the white pine cone as their state "flower" to claiming

Moxie as their official state drink. And, of course, nothing's more fun than confusing first-time tourists with friendly signs pointing them north to Down East.

Q If Philadelphia has such a high crime rate, why is it called "The City of Brotherly Love"?

A In 2007, Philadelphia's murder rate jumped to a twenty-year high of more than one per day, outpacing New York, Los Angeles, and Chicago. So it might seem odd that Philadelphia literally means "The City of Brotherly Love." The name derives from the Greek *philos* ("love") and *adelphos* ("brother").

Philadelphia was founded more than three hundred years ago specifically to serve as an example of how to live peacefully. The year was 1681, and Charles II of England had a debt to repay to the father of William Penn, a Quaker who wished to come to America to escape religious persecution. As you might imagine, when the King of England owes your dad money, you're going to end up with a pretty sweet going-away present.

Charles saw fit to provide William Penn with a huge tract of land across the Atlantic Ocean, west of New Jersey. The king also granted Penn a charter for what became the colony of Pennsylvania. The land was called Sylvania, which is Latin for "woods," and "Penn" was added by Charles in honor of William's father.

Though he had been awarded the land, Penn nonetheless purchased it for £1,200 (which was then considered a handsome price) from the local Lenni Lenape (Delaware) tribe in order to ensure peace and harmony with Native Americans. Penn signed a treaty of friendship with Lenape chief Tammany in what is now Penn Treaty Park in Philadelphia's Kensington neighborhood. In light of his own persecution, Penn founded Pennsylvania on a promise of religious freedom, and god-fearing people of all faiths quickly populated his colony.

Penn envisioned his colony being anchored by a settlement on the Delaware River, which would facilitate trade and make a logical seat of government. He named this capital Philadelphia, and he imbued the city with his personal sense of peace and harmony. For example, Penn refused to increase the size of Philadelphia through uncivil actions, which were prohibited by his Quaker faith. If he wanted land, he displayed uncommon civility for the era and attempted to buy it from the rightful owners.

Penn's son and successor, Thomas, fought to restrict many of the religious freedoms that his father provided in Pennsylvania and became an enemy of Benjamin Franklin in the latter's quest to lead America to independence. How Philadelphia descendants might have lost their way three centuries later is anyone's guess, but in a city whose football fans are infamous for pelting Santa Claus with snowballs, Utopia is a distant memory.

Chapter Eleven

HEALTH MATTERS

Q Do men age better than women?

A When it comes to crow's feet, laugh lines, and permanently furrowed brows, men do age better than women. And there's a scientific reason why Harrison Ford looks better than Carrie Fisher. Turns out men literally have thicker skin than women, and thicker skin is better able to withstand the wrinkles that come with age.

According to Cleveland-based dermatologic surgeon Rebecca Tung, men's skin is 20 to 30 percent thicker than women's, on average. Why? Men's facial skin is built up with more collagen and elastin fibers. These are the connective-tissue fibers that give skin its strength, elasticity, and ability to bounce back. Men's thicker skin is also supported by a tighter network of underlying fatty tissue.

Men have another thing going for them: facial hair. Though guys may tire of the daily shave (and the occasional bloody nick), those tiny hair follicles help create a sort of light-frame construction for the face. Shaving also exfoliates the outer layers of the skin. And because hair glands produce oil, says Seth Yellin—a facial plastic surgeon in Atlanta—men's faces are naturally more hydrated, plump, and youthful in appearance.

Do men really age better than women? Well, even if they're not as likely to blow their retirement fund on Buf-Pufs, Botox, or two hundred-dollar cold creams, men's thicker, oilier skin does make them more susceptible to skin problems such as acne and blackheads. Maybe that's why old guys are so grumpy.

Q What does a rabbit's death have to do with pregnancy?

A Well before at-home pregnancy test kits were available on drugstore shelves, women relied on rabbits to find out if it was time to knit baby booties and stock up on pickles. And you thought having to pee on a little stick was weird!

The rabbit's unwilling role in family planning goes back to the 1920s, when scientists identified human chorionic gonadotropin (hCG) as a hormone that is produced by an embryo and is present in the urine and blood of a pregnant woman. Additional research showed that injecting a pregnant woman's urine into a female lab animal, like a rabbit, made the animal ovulate. At first, medical technicians had to kill and dissect the rabbit to examine its ovaries, but scientists later developed techniques that allowed them to examine the ovaries of living animals.

For several decades, this was the only test that was available to confirm a pregnancy. Women who thought that they might be pregnant went to the doctor's office and provided a urine sample that was sent to a lab. The test wasn't perfect—it took a couple of days to complete, and it wasn't always reliable when the pregnancy was in its early stages. The test was also costly, so many people couldn't afford it.

Everyone pretty much knew that rabbits were somehow involved in the test, but many people were under the impression that a pregnant woman's urine would actually kill a rabbit, so it became common to ask an anxious woman or her spouse, "Did the rabbit die?" In the 1960s, rabbits lost their unenviable place in pregnancy testing when scientists developed a procedure to use human cells to test for hCG. Women started going to doctors' offices for blood tests to determine pregnancy, and in 1978 the first at-home pregnancy test hit the market. Meanwhile, female rabbits went back to doing what they do best: making babies of their own.

Q If you eat a Big Mac every day, are you asking for health problems?

A Nutritionists will tell you that a healthy diet includes a wide variety of grub from all of the food groups. But for

Wisconsin native Don Gorske, variety comes in the form of "two all-beef patties, special sauce, lettuce, cheese, pickles, onions on a sesame seed bun." Since May 17, 1972, Gorske's diet has included a Big Mac every day—actually, two Big Macs, a Coke, and sometimes an order of fries or a parfait.

Talk about a total McTubby! Well, not exactly. The six-foot-two Gorske weighs in at a svelte 185 pounds. He walks an average of ten miles a day and even finished a marathon in 2006. But nobody knows what this modern-day Hamburglar looks like on the inside, so don't go thinking he's any kind of poster child for health.

Gorske typically skips breakfast and lunch (a big metabolic no-no). Furthermore, his daily burger binge is fed by a bona fide obsessive-compulsive disorder. He carries a pocketbook to jot down the details of every single Big Mac that goes down his hatch. Big Mac number 17,355, consumed in Kearney, Nebraska, was the best he's ever had.

There's something to be said for a fifty-four-year-old guy who's gobbled more than twenty-three thousand Big Macs, all the while avoiding a whopper of a coronary (or two). Is this guy an enigma, or is he the human embodiment of Mayor McCheese? Because the facts are these: One Big Mac contains 540 calories, 29 grams of fat (10 of which are saturated), 75 milligrams of cholesterol, and 1,040 milligrams of sodium. It's essentially artery-clogging cardiovascular disease in a box. You want that to go?

Hey, why not? Two of France's best-known nutritionists, Jean-Michel Cohen and Patrick Sérog, have said that the Big Mac is a considerably healthier option than the classic quiche lorraine. They gave *Le Big Mac* a seal of approval in their 2004 good food guide, *Savoir Manger*. According to Cohen and Sérog, Big Macs have a good protein-to-fat ratio and "also have a very filling effect on the stomach, which is good." Anyone smell a French-fried conspiracy?

Q Can worms cure allergies?

A In the dark ages of medicine, the leech—that sloppy, sludgy parasite that looks sort of like a worm on steroids—was used as a tool to fight illness. Of course, we know better now—our high-tech medical remedies are synthesized in sterile labs, not dredged up from muddy lakes. Right?

Not exactly. It turns out that disgusting parasites may still be useful in treating certain conditions that have baffled modern medicine (more useful, in fact, than leeches, which were never really an effective remedy). In 2004, Dr. David Pritchard, an immunologist at Britain's University of Nottingham, deliberately infected himself with hookworms as part of an experiment concerning allergies. And it worked.

Hookworms are nasty little parasites. An untreated infestation can lead to severe anemia and even death. Hookworms are common in undeveloped tropical countries, where it just so happens that allergies are relatively rare. In the developed world, the problems are just the opposite: Few people need to worry about parasitic worms, but allergies are more and more common, causing at least two million emergency room visits each year.

While conducting research in Papua New Guinea, Pritchard began to wonder if this was more than coincidence. Are worms a key to preventing allergies? To test his hypothesis, he gave a group of villagers pills to kill their worms and asked if, in return, they would give him what he politely termed their "fecal matter" to study. Since Pritchard and his assistants didn't speak the local language, they must have used some interesting gestures to get their point across. But it turned into a win-win situation for both parties—the New Guineans got health care and Pritchard got scientific evidence. By comparing the number of worms eliminated by each patient with the concentration of antibodies in the bloodstream, he could see how worms affected the immune system. Since an allergic reaction is basically the body's attempt to defend itself against a hostile invader, worms must be able to suppress this response in order to survive in the gut.

This ability intrigued Pritchard. People with a lot of allergies have hypersensitive immune systems—perhaps a few worms might lower these from constant states of "red alert" to something more akin to "yellow" or even "green." Back home in Britain, Pritchard infected himself to prove that a small dose of worms was not dangerous to the average healthy Westerner. After that, he was able to obtain funding and thirty willing volunteers for a clinical trial. Within a week, the fifteen subjects who had ingested a mere ten worms each found their allergy symptoms disappearing. The others, who had received a placebo, showed little or no improvement. When word of these results hit online discussion boards, inveterate sneezers began demanding Pritchard's "helminthic therapy" to ease their symptoms.

If you have hay fever but are not keen on ingesting hookworms for relief, wait a few years. Scientists are trying to isolate the specific substance that worms use to disarm allergic reactions and are aiming to produce it in pill form, a much more palatable way to fight allergies than embracing our inner parasites. Hopefully, someday soon, you'll be able to pop one of these pills, get a good night's rest, and be fresh as a pollen-proof daisy by morning.

Q Did the USA ever condone forced sterilization?

A Yes. Starting in the late nineteenth century, many intelligent people endorsed the idea that science could improve the human race. To that end, more than sixty thousand Americans were forcibly sterilized, some as late as 1979. And it was all perfectly legal.

Spurred by Charles Darwin's theory of evolution, scientists began wondering about the next step for the species and whether they could influence it. The idea that technology might hold the key to advances in evolution was embraced by the leading thinkers of the day. By the early twentieth century, the "science" of eugenics (which means, literally, "well born") was being taken seriously.

Joining top scientists in the eugenics movement were such prominent figures as author H. G. Wells, British prime minister Winston

Churchill, and U.S. president Woodrow Wilson. Also on board were the philanthropic Rockefeller Foundation and Carnegie Institute.

Eugenicists compared and ranked the world's races and nationalities. These scientists, most of whom were white, predictably found that Anglo-Saxons were far superior to other, "lower" races. Their findings coincided with the United States imposing limits on immigration that first denied the Chinese and then other Asians and Eastern Europeans.

Intolerance, combined with the idea that American stock could be controlled through selective breeding, created a mindset that was reflected by a flurry of state laws from the 1920s that prohibited marriage of the "defective" or "feebleminded." Starting in 1907, some thirty states legalized sterilization for rapists, drug addicts, alcoholics, and even epileptics. A 1927 U.S. Supreme Court decision in the case of *Buck v. Bell* endorsed these laws by approving the forced sterilization of a woman who was judged a "moral imbecile." More than sixty thousand people underwent forced sterilization between 1920 and 1979 in the United States, some simply because they were blind, deaf, homeless, or orphaned.

The Great Depression refocused attitudes and priorities, and as the racist policies of Nazi Germany were exposed, people were horrified at the murders that were committed by Hitler's followers in the name of racial purity. Support for forced sterilizations eroded in the 1930s, though a few sterilizations of the incarcerated continued into the 1980s. As for the scientists and intellectuals who had once promoted eugenics, most eventually rejected it and many pretended that they never endorsed such a preposterous idea in the first place.

Q Are there still lepers?

A Yes, there are about a quarter-million people worldwide with leprosy. It is found mostly in Southeast Asia and in the Third World countries of Africa and the Americas, although about a hundred cases are diagnosed in the United States each year. Cures for leprosy were developed in the 1960s and 1970s, and over the past fifty years, the number of afflicted has dropped from more than five million (perhaps as high as twenty million, according to some estimates) to the present figure.

For centuries, lepers were shunned: Healthy men and women wouldn't so much as touch a leper because the grotesque disease was believed to be highly contagious. We now know that it's not—in fact, 95 percent of humans are naturally immune to it. Still, it's easy to see why the disease would have been so frightening. Leprosy starts with a small sore on the skin, which often goes numb as the disease begins to infect the peripheral nerves. If untreated, it can, in extreme cases, cripple and blind its victims.

This rarely happens today. Medicines as common as antibiotics are often effective at fighting leprosy. Patients can be cured of the disease in months or years, which has helped to erase much of its stigma. Doctors now avoid using the term "leprosy" because of its negative connotations and instead call it "Hansen's disease," after Norwegian doctor G. H. Armauer Hansen, who discovered the bacteria that causes it in 1873.

What about all of the awful stories relating to the affliction? Most scientists think that the leprosy described in the Bible was a different sickness than the one that exists today. Hansen's disease does not turn the skin white, for example, so the leprosy of the Old Testament was probably a combination of several other ravaging infections, maybe even cancers.

Leper colonies really existed, from the Middle Ages through the twentieth century. Father Damien's famous leper colony in Hawaii and another colony in Carville, Louisiana, housed most of the Americans who were diagnosed with Hansen's disease before treatments were developed, but there used to be many other centers around the world. Since the disease destroys the nerves and tissues of the body, it would have been horrifying to watch a victim succumb to it. Without a cure or a known cause, doctors thought it best to keep victims segregated from the healthy.

Doctors still aren't entirely sure how Hansen's disease is transmitted, though they suspect that the bacteria pass through the respiratory system. But since the treatments are so effective, and since most folks are immune, the search for an answer doesn't seem as pressing as it once did.

Q What exactly is the placebo effect?

A A British pharmaceutical company reported with great fanfare in 2006 that a new drug it had developed for food allergies was remarkably effective. Nearly 75 percent of patients who had taken it during the course of the clinical trial reported ameliorated symptoms. Company execs were less thrilled when data came back from the control group, which had been fed inactive tablets designed to look like the allergy drug: Three-quarters of those patients also reported a drastic reduction in allergy symptoms.

The placebo effect—when patients report marked improvements in symptoms despite taking only inactive drugs—is one of the most bewildering phenomena in modern science. Despite the fact that it goes against everything upon which empirical thought is based, study after study has shown incontrovertible evidence that the mere suggestion that patients are receiving a drug or treatment that will help them somehow does help them. Although the most common placebo effects are seen in vague, somewhat immeasurable conditions—such as depression and chronic fatigue syndrome—cases have been reported of the placebo effect causing measurable physical changes in patients, such as the disappearance of tumors.

What's going on here? Are these symptoms merely psychosomatic? Is it mind over matter? A miracle? The answer is...well, there is no answer as of yet. True skeptics—die-hard empiricists who believe in nothing outside of hard science—attribute the placebo effect to the illness merely running its course. (These same skeptics don't opine on what this implies for the use of expensive pharmaceutical drugs that show only a slightly better success rate.)

But these true skeptics are few and far between. Many scientists agree that the placebo effect is very real—35 to 75 percent of patients who participate in placebo studies have reported its effect. And according to the best theories, the placebo effect truly is a case of mind over matter. The power of suggestion, the expectation of a cure, and the emotional response to a caring doctor's concern have all been forwarded as possible explanations for the placebo effect—which means that the hypnotist who advertises on the bulletin board of your local yoga studio might be on to something.

The acknowledgment of placebo effect has led to new research avenues in medicine, which for many years refused to acknowledge the possibility that anything less than chemicals could heal illness. Of course, for those with a Catholic upbringing, the placebo is something very different: It's a term sometimes used for the evening prayers that are said during Vespers. Catholics may recall many an evening spent in a dimly lit church, singing hymns and chanting prayers in an attempt to save their eternal souls. On second thought, perhaps that isn't so different after all.

Q Why would you want to sleep like a baby?

A Babies have it made. Wouldn't it be great if every time you stirred during the night, someone rushed into your bedroom with a plate of barbecue ribs or a slice of chocolate cake? Sure, the changing part might be a little weird, but the food platters would more than compensate.

There are real reasons for sleep-deprived adults to envy a baby's slumber—that's why the phrase "sleep like a baby" has such a positive connotation. Newborns can sleep up to eighteen hours a day. Even at twelve months, babies are sleeping eleven to fourteen hours a night, with a couple of naps mixed in during the day. And we've all seen how infants and toddlers can grab some shut-eye in the strangest places—at parties, at the ballgame, on a rec room floor, etc.

But there's a flip side to the apparent blissfulness of constant slumber—you can detect strong evidence of it in the bleary eyes of any parent who is raising a newborn: Babies might sleep a lot, but they don't sleep for long. The sleep patterns of babies, particularly those of newborns, are significantly different from those of adults. Oftentimes a newborn won't sleep for more than one or two hours at a stretch, and a lot of that sleep is not particularly deep.

Sleep can be divided into two general categories: rapid eye movement (REM) and non-rapid eye movement (NREM). REM sleep tends to be lighter than the NREM variety. The brain activity that takes place during REM sleep is believed to be essential to the rapid development that goes on in babies' bodies, so wee ones spend more time in the REM stage than adults do. The result is that babies wake more easily. Understandably, they're often not happy about it—and, just as understandably, neither are adults.

So sleeping like a baby isn't all that it's cracked up to be. Maybe it's better to simply act our age (although those food platters do sound enticing).

Q Will you ruin your eyes if you sit too close to the TV?

A The lame joke here is: It may not damage your eyes, but your brain will be toast. All research indicates that you won't damage your eyes if you sit too close to the television.

That's not the full story, though. Prior to about 1968, some television sets emitted low-level radiation, which is never a good thing.

But this nasty side effect has been sorted out, and it is safe to sit near modern TVs. Doctors and mothers, however, still advise against sitting too close to the TV and watching it with no other light source in the room. Mothers dispense these warnings because they're, well, mothers. Doctors do so because they're trying to prevent eye fatigue, which, it is important to note, is different from eye damage.

Each of your eyes has muscles that control the shape of your eye lens and your eye movements. The distance of an object on which you're focusing determines the shape of this lens. If the eye muscles spend too much time making the eye lens focus on a television screen that's two inches from your nose, these muscles get tired and strained. Eyes are resilient, though, and a bit of rest will restore their strength.

Watching TV can also cause headaches, even if you're not sitting close to the boob tube. Many televisions flicker slightly, and some emit a high-pitched whine. Video games can be particularly troublesome: Everything on the screen is moving all the time, which can tire your eyes and throw off your balance (which is controlled in the inner ears). Translation: Playing video games can cause motion sickness. In rare cases, the bright colors and sounds of video games, as well as the frenetic images, can trigger epileptic fits.

But fear not—if you set up good lighting in your TV room and give your eyes an occasional rest, you should be just fine. You can even sit as close to the television as your little heart desires. Just don't block anyone's view—then you'll be asking for some serious trouble.

Q Why do pollen and dust make your nose run?

A Noses like to run, don't they? If the weather is cold, they're off to the races. When flu season hits, they're off to the races. And for a lot of people, if there's dust or pollen floating around, they're off to the races again.

On a good day—and by "good," we mean productive—your nose will create about a quart of mucus, which will slide down your throat without you really noticing. Mucus—in case you weren't paying close attention in biology class—is snot. Mucus is fabulous at trapping the airborne particles that you don't want to breathe in. Germs, pollen, dust, and other bits and bobs get stuck in the gooey, slimy, and generally gross stuff and trickle down into your stomach instead of your lungs, where they could trigger some health problems.

Your nose runs when pollen or dust particles flies in because of allergies, which are often inherited from your parents. Maybe your dad has a wonky gene floating around that hasn't killed him yet, so his body reckons it may be useful and he passes it on to you. Whatever the reason, having an allergy means that you're hypersensitive to certain substances.

So if you're allergic to pollen or dust (and many people are), it means that your body treats these particles like germs. Your nose goes into overdrive in order to keep the particles out of your lungs, producing a heck of a lot more mucus to try to trap all of them. Hence, the snot running from your nose.

But let's focus on the more important question of whether to blow it out or snort it down your throat. It's gross information, but useful to know! In truth, neither route will make much of a difference to your health. Plenty of people go both ways, so the choice is yours.

Chapter Twelve

HISTORY

Q Why did Abraham Lincoln have an air corps?

A On June 18, 1861, Abraham Lincoln received an extraordinary message. "I have the pleasure of sending you this first telegram ever dispatched from an aerial station," his correspondent wrote, noting that from his vantage point, he could see the countryside surrounding Washington, D.C., for fifty miles in any direction. The "station" was an enormous hot-air balloon that was tethered across from the White House and hovering five hundred feet in the air. Thaddeus Lowe, the balloon's operator, had run a telegraph line from the passenger basket down to a ground cable that was connected to both the president and the Union Army War Office.

A self-taught scientist, engineer, and aeronaut, Lowe had been piloting balloons for a decade. He was also an ardent supporter of the Union. He had mounted his balloon demonstration because he wanted to serve his country—not on the ground, like other soldiers, but in the air. One of the Union's greatest fears was that the Confederacy would launch a sneak attack on Washington, D.C., via northern Virginia. Who better to keep an eye on enemy maneuvers, Lowe asked, than a spy in the sky?

Lincoln agreed. A few days later, on June 21, he created the Union Army Balloon Corps and appointed Lowe as its chief. Over the next two years, Lowe made three thousand balloon ascents. His telegraph apparatus relayed crucial information to the ground troops. During the Peninsula Campaign of 1861–62, Lowe alerted General George McClellan to the movements of rebel troops three miles away; it was the first time in history that a commander was able to use aerial intelligence to route an enemy. At the Battle of Fair Oaks (May 31–June 1, 1862), Lowe's messages guided an entrapped Union battalion to safety.

Ever alert for new possibilities, Lowe also commandeered a barge from which he could make balloon ascents over the Potomac River, thus creating the first "aircraft carrier." His constant presence in the sky was such an irritant to the South that he became, according to author Carl Sandburg, "the most shot-at man of the Civil War." Though his balloon sailed too high for Confederate artillery to reach—the craft could climb to five thousand feet—Lowe did have a few close calls. At one point, he actually caught a cannonball in his basket.

Despite his daring, Lowe's balloon corps proved too controversial for the army. Rival balloonists, perhaps jealous of his success, accused him of mismanaging funds. Some generals found the balloons too cumbersome and expensive to transport. In addition, Lowe himself suffered ill health from a bout of malaria. The corps was officially disbanded in August 1863, and a disappointed Lowe returned to civilian life.

His exploits were not forgotten, however. He received the Franklin Institute's Grand Medal of Honor in 1886. A mountain near Pasadena, California, bears his name. And in 1988, he was posthumously inducted into the U.S. Military Intelligence Corps Hall of Fame, the sole balloonist among its honorees. It is a fitting tribute to the nation's original spy in the sky.

Q What is the world's most expensive car?

A Pinpointing the world's most expensive car is a little like trying to keep up with the 1,001-horsepower Bugatti Veyron—it's here and then it's gone.

Take the case of the 2008 Lamborghini Reventon, a mid-engine land missile with razor-edged bodywork inspired by the radar-defeating shape of the F-22 Raptor stealth jet fighter. Named for a renowned matador-killing bull, the Reventon (*reben-ton*) has 650 horsepower and a top speed of 211 miles per hour. When it was introduced at the Frankfurt Motor Show on September 11, 2007, it had a sticker price of a million euros, or $1.4 million at the day's exchange rate. This should have been enough to qualify the Lamborghini Reventon as the world's costliest new car. But in this rarefied realm, a million euros was too little, too late.

At that same Frankfurt show, Bugatti unveiled a special edition of its Veyron supercar called the Pur Sang, which means "thoroughbred" or, literally, "pure blood" in French. Like the standard Veyron (*vay-ron*), the Pur Sang is a hand-built wonder with sixteen cylinders, four turbochargers, two seats, 1,001 horsepower, and a claim to the highest-ever top speed for a production car: 253.2 miles per hour. Running at full throttle, a Bugatti Veyron drains its 26.4-gallon fuel tank in thirteen minutes.

The Pur Sang's main distinction is a body with a clear-coat finish that allows a look at the artistry of the Veyron's aluminum and carbon-fiber construction. Bugatti, the a France-based subsidiary of Germany's Volkswagen, set the car's price at 1.4 million euros, or about $1.9 million. This made the 2008 Bugatti Veyron 16.4 Pur Sang the world's most expensive new car.

But there quickly arose a catch. Bugatti said it was building just five Pur Sangs and announced that all five were sold within a day of the car's unveiling. Standard Veyrons remained available, however, and by March 2008, they were priced at around $1.5 million—the same price the Lamborghini Reventon was then fetching.

So is the world's most expensive car a $1.9 million special edition that's unavailable for sale new? Or is it a Bugatti or Lamborghini that retails for $1.5 million, give or take, depending on exchange rates and how much markup you'll swallow to be the first in your gated community to own one? Or is the world's most expensive car something else entirely?

In May 2008, a 1961 Ferrari 250 GT Spyder California SWB sold at auction in Maranello, Italy, for $10.9 million. The stunning V-12 convertible was once owned by the late actor James Coburn. The companies that handled the sale, Sotheby's and RM Auctions, said that it was the highest price ever paid for a vintage car at auction. However, an RM Auctions spokesman added that other Ferraris have changed hands between private collectors for more than $11 million.

And then there's this: Two Los Angeles brothers who owned a luxury car dealership said that they bought a Mercedes-Benz AMG CLK-GTR open-top two-seater, one of just five produced, in 2002 for $1.7 million. Their purchase gained attention in 2006 when they sued the car's manufacturer, claiming that the 612-horsepower roadster broke down the first time they drove it off the lot. Now that's an expensive lemon.

Q Why do they call it the Dark Ages?

A Okay, so maybe the Roman Empire crumbled and all of its advances in urban refinement—in areas such as agriculture, roads, and sanitation—fell into decline. So maybe a few Germanic tribes accosted southern and western Europe and wreaked a little havoc on the culture and the social order. So maybe there was a plague. Anyone can have a bad half-millennium. Do we have to rub salt into the wound and call the whole affair the Dark Ages?

Actually, modern-day historians generally don't use that term anymore. The period that ran from roughly AD 500 to 1000 is now referred to in less pejorative terms, such as "Late Antiquity" or the "Early Middle Ages." For a while, the term "Dark Ages" was co-opted from its original, negative meaning and was used to refer to the fact that historical detail of the era was a bit sketchy—but that never really caught on.

The notion of a specific period of time that we now know as the Middle Ages originated with Renaissance historians. As the Renaissance got into full swing in the fourteenth century, Italian humanist historians sought to link their movement with the classical philosophical movements of Rome and Greece (beginning around the fifth century BC). They needed a name for the downtime between the two movements, so they called it "the Dark Ages," thumbed their noses at it, and then went about the task of showing how enlightened they were.

Fourteenth-century Italian poet-scholar Petrarch is said to have coined the term "Dark Ages." It doesn't appear that he actually used that exact phrase himself, but he is still credited with introducing the idea of a time when knowledge of the great works of classical antiquity faded into obscurity, with nothing new being offered in its place—even if modern historians strenuously disagree with his dismal assessment.

Q Why is the pirate flag called a Jolly Roger?

A With the 1883 publication of Robert Louis Stevenson's *Treasure Island,* the popular idea of the pirate germinated: a witty rogue with an eye patch, a peg-leg, and a smart-ass parrot, sailing the seven seas under the Jolly Roger, good-naturedly plundering booty and instigating a little plank-walking. Unfortunately for those romantics who long for the swashbuckling days of yore, most of Bob Lou Steve's details aren't particularly accurate.

There is little evidence that something as dramatic as "walking the plank" happened much, and parrots were rarely recorded as ships' mascots. But calling the pirate flag the "Jolly Roger" was one of the details Stevenson got right.

For hundreds of years, ships have hoisted the colors of their home country to let other ships know from where they hail. In the golden age of piracy, pirates used this form of communication as well, though more deviously. Often, pirates would fly flags of certain countries as a form of deception, in order to get close to their prey. Once they were within striking distance, the buccaneers would lower their false flags and raise their own ensigns. These flags varied from pirate to pirate, but they all meant the same thing: "Surrender, hand over your booty, and we will not kill you." Though if the pirates raised a red flag, it meant, "We will kill you and take your booty." (One might say these flags were the original "booty call.")

French pirates most prominently used the red flag as a symbol of imminent death, and among these pirates, such a flag became known as a *joli rouge* ("pretty red"). The English, hewing to their long tradition of making no effort to correctly pronounce foreign words, turned this into the "Jolly Roger."

Another theory points to a legendary Tamil pirate by the name of Ali Raja. Raja ruled the Indian Ocean and had such a reputation that even English seamen had heard of the pirate captain. It's not hard to imagine how Europeans who were unfamiliar with Middle Eastern languages might corrupt "Ali Raja" into "Jolly Roger."

The least interesting hypothesis points to the fact that in England during piracy's glory days, the devil was often referred to as "Old Roger." That, combined with the grinning appearance of the skull symbol, led to the flag being called the "Jolly Roger." Unfortunately, there is no definitive evidence that supports one theory over another.

The origin of the familiar skull-and-crossbones image is also unclear. The image had been used as a general symbol of death long before pirates appropriated it—crusaders used the symbol in the 1100s, for example. The first recorded use of the skull-and-crossbones on a pirate flag was in 1700, when a French buccaneer named Emmanuel Wynne hoisted it. After that, the black flag with a variation of the image appeared more frequently and sometimes included hourglasses, spears, and dancing skeletons.

Once Stevenson published *Treasure Island,* the skull-and-crossbones—along with the mythical parrot—became forever associated with pirates in the popular mind. The novel is also famous for introducing the phrase, "Yo, ho, ho, and a bottle of rum" into pirate lore. We don't know what that means, either.

Q Were Pocahontas and John Smith lovers?

A Yikes, let's hope not—the girl was around twelve or thirteen years old when they met. Get the Disney cartoon babe out of your head—the Indian princess was a child and, for all we know, couldn't even sing. So what's the real, unvarnished story of how Pocahontas met Captain John Smith?

Smith was in his mid- to late twenties when he joined the Jamestown expedition, in which more than one hundred English settlers crossed the Atlantic in three small ships in 1607. They sought to establish the first economically viable English colony in the New World, meaning that they'd chop wood and mine precious metals to be sent back to England. They settled in the Chesapeake Bay area and called their camp Jamestown. At the time, most of what is now eastern Virginia was part of the Powhatan Empire, an organized, militaristic state made up of tribes that were under the control of Chief Powhatan, Pocahontas's dad.

Most of the English were unprepared for hardship. When things went bad for the new colony, Smith did his best to hold it together. He learned the language of the Powhatans, bartered for food, and forced his colonists to work and farm. On one of his food-bartering trips, he was taken prisoner and was brought to mighty Powhatan. The chief interrogated him while men armed with clubs watched and waited.

Powhatan decided that Smith should die, and the Englishman was forced to lay his head against a stone. Out came the clubs. Then—as you probably have heard—Pocahontas rushed forward and put her own head over his so that no blows would be delivered. Her father decided to spare Smith's life.

Why did she do it? That's the million-dollar question. She might have been infatuated with the visitor, or she might have wanted the copper bells and beads that he carried as gifts. Another explanation is that Pocahontas and the unwitting Smith were part of a performance or ritual—perhaps to adopt him into the tribe, a typical Indian custom.

Smith himself believed that Pocahontas was simply a compassionate person. And since all we know of the incident came from Smith, we'll have to take him at his word.

Q Why does the American flag have stripes?

A The American flag is one of the most recognizable symbols of the United States, with its fifty white stars set against a blue field and its thirteen horizontal stripes of alternating red and white. Known variously as "Old Glory," "The Star-Spangled Banner," and "The Stars and Stripes," the U.S. flag has undergone a number of design changes over the course of American history. The stripes, however, have pretty much remained in place from the beginning.

Although it's unclear who originally designed the flag, evidence suggests that it was Francis Hopkinson, a signer of the Declaration of Independence, in the late 1770s. Today, each of the flag's fifty stars represents a state. (The number of stars has accounted for most of the revisions to the flag, as the count had to be updated every time a new state joined the union.) Originally, the stripes followed the same concept: Each stripe was to represent a colony, and that number was thirteen when the nation was born.

The Flag Act, dated June 14, 1777, laid out the initial guidelines for flagmakers: "Resolved, that the flag of the United States be thirteen stripes, alternate red and white; that the union be thirteen stars, white in a blue field representing a new constellation." In May of 1795, the numbers were changed to fifteen stars and fifteen stripes, but a later act, signed in 1818, established the format we have today: The flag would have no more than thirteen stripes, but a star would be added for each state in the union.

Thank goodness for the limit on stripes. Imagine the consequences: The flag would either be three stories high or have stripes so thin that you'd need a magnifying glass to tell one from another.

Q What was the first synthetic fabric?

A Did you guess nylon? If so, give yourself half a point. Nylon, invented by DuPont scientist Wallace Carothers in 1935, was the first fabric made from nonorganic sources. Water-resistant, strong, and stretchy, nylon was a big hit. DuPont spent seven years and twenty-seven million dollars tweaking its "new silk," which revolutionized the hosiery industry.

But the first true synthetic fabric was rayon, which was introduced back in 1884. Rayon is made from a naturally occurring polymer. And what exactly does that mean? Well, cellulose—which is plant fiber, the most common organic substance on the planet—is technically a polymer. To chemists, this means cellulose is made of molecules that are arranged in repeated units and are connected by covalent chemical bonds.

Cellulose turns into nitrocellulose when it's exposed to nitric acid. Nitrocellulose can be used in explosives, and we all know how men like to play with explosives. Around 1855, Swiss chemist Georges Audemars was playing, or "experimenting," with nitrocellulose and discovered that certain solvents made it break down into fibers that looked a lot like silk. He called his new fabric "artificial silk," but as it had a tendency to explode, he didn't sell much of it.

Frenchman Hilaire de Chardonnet—the Count of Chardonnet—took the invention further and patented his "Chardonnay silk" in 1884. He made the material from the pulp of mulberry trees, because silk worms fed on mulberry leaves. Soft and pretty, Chardonnay silk didn't explode, though it did have a nasty habit of bursting into flames. In the days of fireplaces and floor heaters that were fueled by gas, ladies were naturally a little nervous about wearing something so flammable. The fabric, initially popular, was banned in several countries.

In 1892, English scientists Charles Cross, Edward Bevan, and Clayton Beadle figured out how to cheaply and safely make artificial silk that didn't catch fire so easily. Their product was called viscose, and it hit U.S. stores in 1910. A committee of textile manufacturers and the folks at the U.S. Department of Commerce held a contest to rename the fabric in 1924. The winning name? Rayon, which is possibly a combination of "ray" (the fabric's sheen may have reminded folks of a ray of sunshine) and the "on" from "cotton."

Q Why was smallpox so deadly for Indians, but not Europeans?

A The Europeans were not good guests in the New World. Whether it was conquistadores in the Caribbean, Pilgrims in New England, sailors in Fiji, or settlers in Australia, they left a calling card no one wanted: diseases that killed thousands of people. Some experts think that smallpox and other diseases, such as measles and influenza, killed up to 95 percent of the native populations of these locales—in other words, only one in twenty people survived.

Yet the Europeans remained ridiculously healthy. And when they sailed back home, they brought no new illnesses with them. Why?

The Europeans had already been exposed to epidemic diseases—or at least their ancestors had. Smallpox was known in ancient Egypt, and a smallpox epidemic killed millions of Romans in the second century AD. The disease hit Europe so frequently that the folks who had no natural immunities died off. Those who lived passed their immunities on to their children. Over the centuries, with so many nasty plagues hitting big population centers, the surviving Europeans became more resistant to the killer microbes.

Where did these diseases originate? Was there a Patient Zero? No. Most of the epidemic bugs—smallpox, measles, influenza, and even tuberculosis—came from livestock. When Asians and Europeans began herding cattle and penning up ducks and pigs thousands of years ago, they breathed in the strange germs that hung around the animals. Once humans started living in cities in large numbers, these germs were able to spread like wildfires. Europe suffered through the same plagues that killed so many Indians and islanders, but Europe's experience took place hundreds of years earlier, and its populations recovered.

The conquistadores, Pilgrims, sailors, and settlers who crossed the seas during the Age of Exploration came from families that had survived waves and waves of disease. Without realizing it, they brought smallpox, measles, and influenza germs with them to infect people who had never seen cattle, never herded animals, and never, ever been exposed to any of these diseases.

You know the result: Millions died. How many millions is unknown because experts aren't sure about the sizes of pre-encounter populations. The first wave of smallpox to hit Mexico's Aztec Empire in 1520 killed half the kingdom. Up to ten million died, including the emperor. More disease followed, and a century later, the area's native population numbered only 1.6 million.

Here's another infamous example: In 1837, smallpox hit the Mandan, an Indian tribe in North Dakota. The disease, brought by someone who was on a steamboat traveling up the Missouri River, almost destroyed the tribe. Within weeks, the Mandan population of one village dropped from two thousand to forty.

And since no one back then knew about germs, microbes, or how sicknesses spread, the Europeans weren't even aware of what they'd done.

Q Why did men in colonial times wear those silly white wigs?

A You can credit—or blame it on—Louis XIII of France and his premature baldness. He donned a wig in 1624 at age twenty-three to cover up his dome, and by mid-century, wigs were a staple of court fashion for the middle and upper classes in both France and England.

In the case of Louis—and his son, Louis XIV, who carried both his father's genetic predisposition to baldness and his taste in head-wear—the wigs were long, flowing, and curly. If you're turning up your nose at this, then please explain your affection for 1980s hair bands like Mötley Crüe, Dokken, Poison, and Quiet Riot.

Long, abundant hair on men has been considered manly since at least Biblical times (see the story of Samson, for example), and the early white wigs were—in their own way—manly. What is harder to explain is the shorter and more oddly shaped wigs of the eighteenth century, which made their way to North America along with the settlers.

Part of the explanation is expediency. Today we take for granted what the average stylist at Supercuts can do for us at a moment's notice for about fifteen bucks. But three hundred years ago, it wasn't that easy. In addition to the time and cost of hair care, there were scourges like lice to worry about. Tara Maginnis, a fashion expert for Costumes.org, says that men chose wigs for "ease of hairdressing (send your hair out to be done, and you don't have to sit for hours in curlers), ease of cleaning (if you got lice you could boil your wig and shave your head and—zip—no lice), comfort while sleeping (short hair beneath), ability to change styles/color as easily as putting on a hat, and class considerations (wigs were expensive and looked it)."

By the time men's wigs fell out of favor in the late eighteen hundreds they had been through myriad changes in shape and size and often had been dyed various colors, not just white. Protestant and Catholic clergy preferred certain types of wigs, as did barristers (lawyers who handled matters in court) and others. Posh parties called for their own special wigs, which were usually more flowing, full, and curly.

There's another way to answer this question, which is to state the obvious: What appears sexy to one generation or culture can appear grotesque to another. Consider how off-putting the clothing that you wore a decade ago seems to you now.

Q What was the Rape of Nanking?

A This menacing phrase refers to the brutal mass murders, arson, rapes, and pillaging that took place in Nanking (now called Nanjing), China, from December 1937 to February 1938. The victims were mostly Chinese, both civilians and soldiers, and the aggressors were the invading Japanese army. Between two hundred and fifty thousand and three hundred thousand people were killed.

Here's the background: Japan invaded and occupied Manchuria, in northeastern China, in 1931. Meeting no real opposition, Japan renamed the province Manchukuo and made plans to expand Japanese power in Asia. At the time, a worldwide economic depression preoccupied many countries (including the United States), and fascist dictatorships were on the rise in Europe.

Air raids over Nanking began in the brutally hot summer of 1937. By November, Japan announced that a million soldiers had landed and were marching on Nanking, which was the capital of the Republic of China and a major port on the Yangtze River.

The claim may have been true—there might actually have been a million soldiers. But they were deployed without much food, so looting was encouraged by their officers. Predictably, turning military men lose to pillage led to wanton violence and murders. In addition, the Chinese army surrendered in huge numbers, and the Japanese weren't prepared to keep them captive. It was easier to shoot them than to build prisons for them; in fact, the official Japanese orders were to "take no prisoners."

Rapes and massacres took place before the city of Nanking fell in mid-December. Survivors told of seeing their homes burned and their families—even children—gunned down. Girls were gang-raped and killed. Then the real horrors began.

The Japanese started a campaign of absolute terror against the Chinese. Innocent people were mowed down by machine guns as they tried to flee the city, and so were the soldiers who surrendered. Mass murders—not of hundreds of people but of *thousands*—became common. In one case, both survivors and Japanese soldiers told of the killing of up to twenty thousand Chinese troops in one day. Other diaries and interviews described grenades being thrown into crowds, poison gas clouds, and rows and rows of civilians being bayoneted.

Soon, mountains of bodies lined the roads. The carcasses clogged the waterways, as well; one soldier called the Yangtze a "river of corpses." A destroyed bridge near Nanking's Shuixi Gate was replaced by bodies that were thrown into the river until they were piled so high that they formed a new bridge. Doors and planks were arranged on top so that the "bridge" could be crossed.

By February 1938, gangs of laborers were burying or burning the bodies, and the worst of the bloodshed was over. Today, the Rape of Nanking stands out as a black mark on the history of humankind.

Q Why did Pilgrims wear buckles on their hats?

A Thanksgiving is a special time of year. Americans gather around the holiday table to eat, drink, and give thanks. We're grateful for our health, our families, the bounty we're about to receive, and, most of all, for the evolution of fashion.

Why are we thankful fashion has evolved? Because we associate Thanksgiving with Pilgrims, and in the popular mind, Pilgrims dressed like deranged leprechauns: black pants, white collars, conical hats, buckles, buckles, and more buckles. Buckles on the shoes make a certain sense. Buckles on the belt are understandable. But why in the world did Pilgrims need buckles on their hats?

Actually, Pilgrims didn't wear buckles on their hats—or any-where else, for that matter. Most Pilgrims didn't wear black and white on a regular basis, either. The misconception that Pilgrims dressed dourly and had a buckle fetish is rooted in a long and proud tradition of Americans misunderstanding and misinterpret-ing their past.

It's time for a quick refresher on colonial history. The New England colonies were settled by two distinct groups of British colonists, the Pilgrims and the Puritans. Both the Pilgrims and the Puritans came to the New World because of religion, but they were decid-edly different types of people.

The Pilgrims, led by William Bradford, came first, arriving on the *Mayflower* in Plymouth in 1620. They left England in search of religious freedom. The Pilgrims were separatists who wanted to break completely from the Anglican Church. These were the people who celebrated the first Thanksgiving.

The Puritans didn't arrive until 1630. They settled in Salem and founded the city of Boston. The Puritans were high-minded Anglicans who believed that the Anglican Church as it stood in England was corrupt and sinful. They came to the New World seeking to establish a "City on a Hill," a religious settlement. The Puritans never intended to break with the Anglican Church—they merely wanted to purify it.

Popular history has conflated the two groups, so when most Americans envision the early colonists, they imagine the drab black-and-white clothing the Puritans wore on special occasions. The Pilgrims rarely wore such clothing, preferring dyed violet, green, burgundy, brown, and other rich hues.

But what about the buckles? Neither group wore buckles on hats. Fashion historians date the popularity of buckles on hats (a short-lived trend) to the late seventeenth and early eighteenth centuries—a good eight decades after the Pilgrims celebrated the first Thanksgiving. Some historians suggest that the buckle motif found its way into portrayals of Pilgrims created during the late nineteenth century, when Thanksgiving became a national holiday and illustrators scrambled to depict the first Thanksgiving in popular media and children's books.

So next Thanksgiving, leave your buckled hat in the closet. But keep your belt buckle—you'll need something to loosen at the end of the meal.

Chapter Thirteen

ORIGINS

Q Where did the thumbs-up come from?

A Long before the box-office fate of a movie rested on the opposable digits of Siskel and Ebert, the thumbs-up enjoyed a rich and colorful history. The act of indicating favor or disfavor by raising or lowering the thumb is thousands of years old.

Most historians agree that the thumbs-up began in ancient Rome. Because there was no television or soccer, watching people kill each other was the dominant form of entertainment. The contestants, known as gladiators, fought in public arenas, the most notable of which was the Colosseum in Rome. Once a gladiator was defeated, the victorious warrior looked to the crowd to determine his opponent's fate. Back then, the thumbs-up meant, "Kill 'em." (Many historians believe that the thumb was stuck outward, not upward.) The extended thumb symbolized the gladiator's sword, as in, "Take it out and behead this loser!"

It wasn't until World War II that the thumbs-up began to connote something a bit more upbeat. United States pilots used the thumbs-up to signal to the ground crew that they were ready for take-off. Journalists documenting the war captured these moments, and the gesture was picked up by GIs who were marching toward Germany. Soon, the thumbs-up spread across Europe.

Sadly, despite its epic origins, the thumbs-up now seems to be most commonly associated with drunken frat brothers posing for pictures above the inert form of a passed-out pledge. If only they knew the Roman meaning of the thumbs-up and were able to appreciate the delicious irony.

Q Why would anyone want to be the devil's advocate?

A Any plan that can't survive scrutiny deserves to fail, and it's the role of the devil's advocate to ferret out the flaws and shine a light on them. This isn't being needlessly argumentative. It's a hallowed responsibility—some might say a sacred one.

Nonetheless, it can be a thankless job. When it comes to exposing foibles, there's a fine line between an honorable adversary and a horse's ass. But what's the devil got to do with it?

During the Renaissance, the Catholic Church needed a few good skeptics. In 1587, Pope Sixtus V created a judicial procedure for canonizing saints. Canonization required proof that the nominee had performed at least two miracles. One priest was chosen to present arguments against conferring sainthood—his task was to examine evidence thoroughly and note any sign that the miracles in question were not of a divine nature and could be explained by natural causes. To many Catholics, this was like taking Satan's side against faith and religious belief—it was like being the devil's advocate.

To its credit, the Vatican considered the role to be one of distinction and honor. The official title of the "devil's advocate" was *Promoter Fidei* ("Promoter of the Faith"). By challenging the faith, the advocate was actually strengthening it and, in the process, weeding out the less than saintly. One priest, Prospero Lambertini, worked as *Promoter Fidei* for twenty years; he then won a big promotion and ruled as Pope Benedict XIV from 1740 to 1758. Pope John Paul II eliminated the role of the devil's advocate in 1983. It was a controversial decision that left many Catholics wondering if the church had lowered the bar for sainthood.

The merits of a devil's advocate extend beyond religious matters, of course. Brazilian business consultant and mathematician Marcial Losada studies how groups make decisions, and he values the role of the devil's advocate. Losada notes, for example, that if no one at a marketing meeting likes a new product, but everyone goes along with it anyway in order to please the boss, the product is likely doomed. A new gizmo that is unanimously beloved is just as likely to fail, he says, if no one in the group steps up to scrutinize it for flaws before it goes to market.

Being a mathematician, Losada has reduced the dilemma to a formula called the "Losada Line." Basically, according to Losada's theory, every decision-making group needs a positive-to-negative ratio of almost three-to-one to succeed. In other words, for roughly every three yea-sayers, a business needs one naysayer as a reality check. So if you're a devil's advocate, stand up and be counted. Consider it your sacred duty.

Q What happens if you lose your mojo?

A "I got my mojo working," sings blues legend Muddy Waters. But what if you're not as fortunate as old Muddy? Lose your mojo and you could be in for a heap of hurt.

A staple in blues music for a good century now and among the tenets of African and African American branches of spirituality and witchcraft called hoodoo, mojo is a kind of power. It's embodied in a charm or group of charms and is often enclosed in a small cloth bag. Mojo is the spirit; mojo hand is the group of items that embody the mojo; and mojo bag is the delivery system.

Believers who want to cast a spell on someone seek out a hoodoo conjurer or witch doctor to create the mojo hand and bag. The conjurer anoints the mojo with some kind of oil or bodily fluid. The mojo is set to work by placing the bag near the intended victim. If the mojo works, the person behaves in the way the believer wants. If the target realizes that the mojo is at work, he or she can employ a witch doctor to break the spell or use hoodoo methods to destroy the mojo.

In America, these beliefs and customs were strongest in the Deep South, and were most common in the nineteenth and early twentieth centuries. Today, mojo is more than just a beloved theme of the blues—it's spread beyond its old hoodoo connotations to mean sexual power or just about any other vague, desirable personal quality. In fact, its vagueness is part of its strength. It allows us to say, "I just don't have my mojo today" or "She's just got a kind of mojo." Even someone who's never heard of Muddy Waters is likely to understand.

And if you lose your mojo? Do what sufferers have traditionally done: Head for the witch doctor or fight back with your own hoodoo. Today's witch doctors come in many forms, from your personal trainer, to your shrink, to your best friend. And hoodoo might be a long walk in the woods, a favorite mix CD—heck, even your copy of *Vogue*. If you believe in the power of mojo, the key to getting it back is having faith that you can.

Q How can a bell save you?

A "Saved by the bell" is a phrase that's uttered in times of great relief, when something intervenes at the very moment all hope seems lost. For example: An unprepared student is stuttering and searching for a response to the teacher's question, then sighs thankfully as he hears the end-of-period bell. But where did this phrase originate?

Probably boxing, where a bell is rung at the beginning and the end of each round. Sportswriters toward the end of the nineteenth century began using the phrase to describe a boxer who had been beaten to a pulp but was saved, at least temporarily, from certain annihilation by the clanging of the end-of-round bell.

There is another, more interesting potential origin of the phrase, although it has little basis in fact. It goes something like this: In medieval times, folks drank by lead cups. Their drinks would become contaminated by the toxic metal, and when the revelers passed out, they would go into a so-called lead coma. To doctors of the day, with their limited knowledge and medical equipment, these people appeared to be dead. So, accordingly, they were sealed in wooden coffins and buried. Discovery of these mistakes came much later, when the coffins were dug up and examined. The inside lids were marked with deep scratches from the prematurely buried, who had desperately tried to break out.

Such incidents fostered a fear of being buried alive and led to the invention of the "safety coffin." This puppy came with a tube, which protruded from the surface of the gravesite, attached to the lid. A bell was located at the top of the tube; a string hung down so that, upon awakening, the not-quite-deceased could ring the bell and be saved.

Research shows that the safety coffin really did exist; a record of the 1868 patent request by Franz Vester of New Jersey for this lifesaver is reproduced in the book *Mad Inventions*. However, there's no evidence that any bell ringing actually occurred.

So if you want accuracy regarding the origin of the phrase in question, look to the boxing ring. But if you want a great story, take a gander at the safety coffin.

Q How did Murphy get his own law?

A Murphy's Law holds that if anything can go wrong, it will. Not surprisingly, the most widely circulated story about the origin of Murphy's Law involves a guy named Murphy.

In 1949, Captain Edward A. Murphy, an engineer at Edwards Air Force Base in California, was working on Project M3981. The objective was to determine the level of sudden deceleration a pilot could withstand in the event of a crash. It involved sending a dummy or a human subject (possibly also a dummy) on a high-speed sled ride that came to a sudden stop and measuring the effects.

George E. Nichols, a civilian engineer with Northrop Aircraft, was the manager of the project. Nichols compiled a list of "laws" that presented themselves during the course of the team's work. For example, Nichols's Fourth Law is, "Avoid any action with an unacceptable outcome."

These sled runs were repeated at ever-increasing speeds, often with Dr. John Paul Stapp, an Air Force officer, in the passenger seat. After one otherwise-flawless run, Murphy discovered that one of his technicians had miswired the sled's transducer, so no data had been recorded. Cursing his subordinate, Murphy remarked, "If there is any way to do it wrong, he'll find it." Nichols added this little gem to his list, dubbing it Murphy's Law.

Not long after, Stapp endured a run that subjected him to forty Gs of force during deceleration without substantive injury. Prior to Project M3981, the established acceptable standard had been eighteen Gs, so the achievement merited a news conference. Asked how the project had maintained such an impeccable safety record, Stapp cited the team's belief in Murphy's Law and its efforts to circumvent it. The law, which had been revised to its current language before the news conference, was quoted in a variety of aerospace articles and advertisements, and gradually found its way into the lexicon of the military and of pop culture.

It's important to note that "laws" that are remarkably similar to Murphy's—buttered bread always lands face down; anything that can go wrong at sea will go wrong, sooner or later—had been in circulation for at least a hundred years prior to Project M3981. But even if Edward Murphy didn't break new ground when he cursed a technician in 1949, it's his "law" we quote when things go wrong, and that's all right.

Q What are red-letter days?

A You graduate from college. You get married. Your screenplay for *Star Wars: Episode IX—Luke Battles Osteoporosis* catches the eye of George Lucas's maid's second cousin. These are special days, worthy of celebration, days you will remember for the rest of your life. They are known as red-letter days.

Everyone loves a red-letter day (except maybe Hester Prynne from *The Scarlet Letter*). We use the phrase to commemorate milestones in our personal lives. But there is more to red-letter days than that. You might not feel the same way about your anniversary as you do about, say, Saint Swithin's Day (July 15) or the Feast of the Annunciation (March 25), but these, too, are red-letter days—or at least they are red-letter days in the original sense.

That's because the first red-letter days were notable for their religious importance. The phrase was inspired by an age-old tradition that called for calendars to be marked in red ink on saints' days and religious holidays. The practice dates back at least to the fifteenth century; it was known to William Caxton, the first book publisher in England. He printed a book in 1490 in which he wrote, "We wryte yet in oure kalenders the hyghe festes wyth rede lettres of coloure of purpre." (Hey, somebody get this guy a spell-checker!)

Caxton didn't actually use the words "red-letter day," though. That phrase entered the lexicon sometime in the early seventeen hundreds. At first, it referred only to days with religious significance, but its meaning soon expanded to encompass any momentous occasion. By the nineteenth century, the phrase was in common usage, as in this sentence written by Victorian novelist Anthony Trollope in 1887: "I used to dine and pass the evening with Dr. Jeune; and these were my red-letter days." These sound like boring days to us, but to each his own.

Q How bad did you have to be to be forced to walk the plank?

A You wouldn't necessarily have had to be bad at all. The instigators of plank-walkings—those guys who were brandishing their swords at your back and compelling you along on your fatal journey off the side of the boat—were usually pirates and mutineers. In other words, they were guys who weren't exactly known for their commitment to fairness and justice.

One of the earliest definitions of the phrase "walking the plank" appears in the 1788 book *A Classical Dictionary of the Vulgar Tongue,* which explains it as "a mode of destroying devoted persons or officers in a mutiny on ship-board." The victim was bound and blindfolded and forced to walk on a board that was balanced on the ship's side until he fell into the water. This way, "as the mutineers suppose," they might avoid the penalty for murder. Since no record exists of charges being brought against anyone who forced their officers to walk the plank, maybe those old scalawags were right.

On the other hand, it's possible that plank-walking was an extremely rare occurrence—if it ever really happened at all. In fact, some experts scoff at the notion, saying that the practice existed only in the work of novelists and illustrators. But journalists wrote about it, too. In 1821, a Jamaican newspaper reported that pirates from a schooner had boarded the English ship *Blessing.* When the pirates were unable to get any money out of the *Blessing*'s captain, their leader made him walk the plank. The buccaneers then shot the ousted captain three times as he struggled to stay above the water before musket-whipping the captain's teenage son, pitching him overboard, and setting the entire ship aflame. (Now that's a thorough job!) Another sailor, George Wood, confessed a similar crime to a chaplain just before being hanged for mutiny in 1769. No other documentation exists to validate either story.

Where did the idea of walking the plank originate? It's possible that it was conjured by the pirates who plagued the Mediterranean Sea when it was dominated by the Roman Empire. Yes, there were pirates in those days, and when they captured Roman ships, they would mock the citizens by telling them that they were free to walk home. Of course, at sea, there's no place to walk without sinking like a stone.

But if walking the plank wasn't actually used as a form of maritime punishment, how were unwanted men dealt with at sea? Marooning—leaving a man on a desert island to die—was a popular practice among both pirates and mutineers. In addition, prisoners were tied up and tossed overboard to drown or be eaten by sharks. Eyewitness accounts of hanging, shooting, whipping, and torturing prisoners abound. Fun guys, those pirates.

Q For Pete's sake, who is Pete?

A Darn. Shoot. Friggin'. You probably recognize these words for what they are: wimpy substitutes for the obscenities many of us call upon when our verbiage needs some added octane. These faux obscenities are uttered after hitting one's thumb with a hammer, or when watching the other team's pitcher hit a two-out grand slam. You get the idea.

It appears as if the Pete in "for Pete's sake" is one of these polite, euphemistic replacements used by the more restrained among us. Like "gosh" and "jeez," "Pete" is a stand-in that allows the speaker to express extra emotion without taking the Lord's name in vain.

Why Pete? Who the hell—um, heck—is this guy? Some believe he's Saint Peter. Others think he's not a particular Pete but rather an offshoot of the saying "for pity's sake."

Whoever he is, we can probably assume that he's not the same Peter, who, along with Dick and Jimmy, belongs to the Johnson family of euphemisms.

Q How did the term "bootleg" come to be associated with illegal activity?

A Coined in the seventeenth century, the term "bootleg" referred to, appropriately enough, the upper part of a boot. But thanks to good old American ingenuity, its meaning subsequently widened.

Bootlegs were handy for concealing all manner of things that a boot-wearer shouldn't have been carrying, from an extra gun to a bowie knife. In the late eighteen hundreds, bootlegs became effective storage places for illicit liquor that was subsequently traded to Native Americans.

The association between the word "bootleg" and the concealment of illegal alcohol was solidified with the onset of prohibition in the United States in 1920. Ships and trucks—which brought foreign-made liquor into the country from Canada, Mexico, the Bahamas, and Cuba—replaced bootlegs, but the intent was exactly the same, and so the name stuck.

As the United States government refined its methods of locating contraband alcohol, the crafty smugglers adjusted, organizing into gangs and directing multifaceted enterprises. In addition to transporting booze, these growing syndicates produced and stored it. "Bootlegging" came to refer to every aspect of the smuggling process.

Prohibition laws were repealed in 1933, but the term "bootleg" has lived on. It is now used to describe any number of nefarious activities. For example, bootlegged booze has given way to bootlegged music. The parallel works just fine, but there is one problem: It's nigh on impossible to hide an illegally downloaded song in a bootleg.

Q How do you pass an acid test?

A Remember the first time you met your girlfriend's father? The interrogation? The stammering? The urge to run away? That was an acid test. No actual acid was involved, of course. But the experience could hardly have been worse had he applied burning chemicals to your skin.

An acid test is administered to gauge authenticity. The term is borrowed from metallurgy, specifically gold mining. A quick way to distinguish real gold from fool's gold is to subject it to an acid test: Real gold doused with acid won't dissolve.

When we pass an acid test, we have proved we are genuine, that our intentions are pure. Indeed, if you got your girlfriend home on time after that first parental encounter, you were golden—at least until the next date.

Now, if your girlfriend's father happened to be Timothy Leary, your acid test might have included vivid colors, incoherent conversation, and uncontrolled laughter. But chances are you wouldn't have remembered much of it.

Chapter Fourteen

MORE GOOD STUFF

Q What exactly is money laundering?

A You knock over an armored car and suddenly your mattress is overflowing with cash. But if you enjoy your ill-gotten gains by treating yourself to something big—solid-gold yacht, say—the Feds will want to know where the money came from. And if you can't point to a legitimate source, it's off to the big house with you.

When faced with this dilemma, criminals turn to money laundering, the process of making "dirty" money look "clean"—in other words, making it appear that the money is legitimate income. For relatively small amounts of dirty cash, the go-to trick is to set up a front: a business that can record the cash as profit. For example, Al Capone owned Laundromats all over Chicago so that he could disguise the income from his illegal liquor business as laundry profits (how appropriate). There wasn't any way to know how much money people really spent at the Laundromat, so all the profit appeared to be legitimate.

On a larger scale—such as when drug traffickers take in millions—the Laundromat scheme doesn't really work, and things get more complicated. But no matter how elaborate the scheme, you can usually break it down into three basic steps: placement, layering, and integration.

In the placement stage, the goal is to get the hard cash into the financial system, which usually means depositing it into accounts of some kind. In the United States, banks report any transaction greater than ten thousand dollars to the authorities, so one placement strategy is to deposit money gradually, in smaller increments, across multiple bank accounts. Another option is to deposit the money in a bank in a country that has lax financial monitoring laws.

The goal of the next stage—layering—is to shift the money through the financial system in such a complicated way that nobody can follow a paper trail back to the crime. In other words, the criminals are trying to disguise the fact that they are the ones who put the money into the financial system in the first place. Every time launderers move money between accounts, convert it into a different currency, or buy or sell anything—particularly in a country with lax laws—the transaction adds a layer of confusion to the trail.

Finally, in the integration stage, the criminals get the money back by some means that looks legitimate. For example, they might arrange to have an offshore company hire them as generously paid consultants; this way, the money that they earned from their crimes enters their bank accounts as legitimate personal income.

Money laundering is big business, and it's a key foundation for drug trafficking, embezzling, and even terrorism. Many nations have enacted stricter laws and boosted enforcement in order to crack down on money laundering, but they can't put a stop to it unless everyone is vigilant. As long as there are countries with lax financial regulations that trade in the world economy, criminals will have a way to launder their funds.

So, if you've been busily scrubbing your ill-gotten cash in the sink and hanging it on the line to dry, you can stop now. You're doing it wrong.

Q Is sign language the same in all languages?

A Nope. There are many different sign languages in use around the world. French-speaking nations have their own sign language, as do Spanish-speaking countries. But that doesn't mean sign language is a sort of gestural translation of the local vernacular. Two countries that share a spoken language—like the United States and England—can end up using completely different signing systems. In fact, American Sign Language actually has more in common with its French counterpart than with British Sign Language. To understand why this is, you have to look at where modern sign languages were developed: in the early schools for the deaf.

The first of these institutions was opened in France in the mid-eighteenth century by Charles-Michel, abbé de l'Epée. Other educators before him had tutored deaf children from well-to-do families, but Charles-Michel sought to help the poorest deaf children, who otherwise would have been pushed to the fringes of society. In his school, he developed a rudimentary system for signing letters and whole words.

In the early nineteenth century, Thomas Gallaudet of Hartford, Connecticut, wanted to establish a school for the deaf in the United States. He raised money and traveled across the Atlantic to observe European teaching methods so that he could emulate them in his own school. The English refused to share their techniques with him, but the French welcomed him. He returned to Connecticut, bringing with him the sign language developed by Charles-Michel, and in 1817, he established the school that is now known as the American School for the Deaf.

The French method of signing that Charles-Michel taught his students gradually spread to schools around the United States. Combined with other local signing systems, it became American Sign Language (ASL), which is a living language—one to which new signs are added—and is among the most complete sign languages in the world.

Linguists estimate that more than half of the signs in French Sign Language and ASL overlap, due to their common origins. It's likely that a deaf person from France and one from the United

States could communicate easily. British Sign Language, on the other hand, has little in common with ASL, so there is a much more profound communication barrier between deaf people from different parts of the English-speaking world.

International Sign Language, formerly known as Gestuno, is used for conferences such as the World Federation of the Deaf and the Deaflympics, but it's a separate language with a unique system of signs. The bottom line? Just like those that are spoken, sign languages are rich, diverse, and expressive.

Q Do Social Security numbers contain a secret code?

A Yes, but as secret codes go, it's duller than dirt. It's also not very secret.

Social Security numbers have nine digits. The first three reveal the geographic area of the holder—or at least the area in which the holder lived when he or she applied for the Social Security number. The digits start low on the East Coast and get higher as you move west. For example, a Social Security number starting with 648 indicates that the card was issued in New Mexico.

This part of the code was designed in the mid-1930s, when Social Security numbers were distributed by individual states. After a state issued a card, the holder's information was sent to be filed at the main Social Security office in Baltimore. This was long before computers, so the geographic coding helped if someone wanted to look up a Social Security number.

Assignment of the middle two numbers is confusing, so let's first address the final four numbers. They are four digits that range from 0001 to 9999.

Now for those pesky middle numbers. In each state, the first 9,999 people are issued cards with middle numbers 01, followed by the four-number sequence mentioned above that ranges from 0001 to 9999. It would seem that after the 01s are exhausted, starting with the 10,000th person, the middle two numbers would be 02. Wrong. After the 01s, the middle numbers that are assigned are, in order, 03, 05, 07, and 09.

After the 09 numbers are exhausted, the middle numbers become 10, followed by even-numbered middle digits up to 98. After all the Social Security numbers that include those middle two digits have been issued, the middle-number sequence goes to the even numbers from 02 to 08. Then comes 11, followed by all the odd numbers up to 99.

Get the feeling that people who were running the Social Security Administration had too much time on their hands? Thankfully, the final four numbers get assigned consecutively as applications for cards roll in—no trick there. And neither the cards nor the numbers are coded to reveal race or other demographic information.

The numbering system may be cumbersome, but it can reveal a bogus Social Security number. For example, those who apply for a card in New Hampshire might get a number starting with 001, followed by odd-numbered middle digits. Most of the even-numbered middle digits have not yet been used, so if a number like 001–96–1234 appears on a Social Security card, that card is clearly a fake.

Q Why do newer car models have letters and numbers instead of names?

A Goodbye, Lincoln Continental; hello, Lincoln MKS. So long, Cadillac Eldorado; *ciao*, Cadillac XLR. *Adios*, Acura Legend; hi there, Acura RL.

What the #@!$ is going on? Why are automakers veering from perfectly good names and toward a jumble of letters and numbers? What exactly is an xB? Or an S34? Where's the Thunderbird when you need it? As it turns out, image enhancement, brand building, and a shortage of great car names are all responsible for this gibberish.

Image is just about everything to an upscale car brand. It's no accident that the automakers most associated with non-word names tend to be the upscale varieties, such as BMW (with its 330i and 760iL, for example) and Mercedes-Benz (C350, S550). These old-line automakers have used alphanumerics for years as codes that are clear once you crack them. The E350, for example, belongs to Mercedes-Benz's E-Class line, which slots between the lower-priced C-Class and top-line S-Class lines; 350 denotes its 3.5-liter engine.

Rivals who were hungry to project premium images imitated this convention, but seldom with much meaning behind the letters or numbers. The RL, TL, TSX, MDX, or RDX on the back of an Acura, for instance, doesn't actually stand for anything, the company admits. Acura says it went with letters in order to emphasize the Acura brand and differentiate its luxury cars from the mainstream wares of parent company Honda.

Some automakers choose alphanumerics to subjugate individual car models to the lord of brand identity. They insist that an owner who's prompted to say "I drive a Lincoln" or "I drive a Cadillac" instead of "I drive an MKZ" or "I drive an STS" is spreading brand recognition. This thinking leads to such badges as the intentionally obtuse MKS from Lincoln and the meaning-challenged SRX from Cadillac. Skeptics of this logic are legion. And some cynics note how fond moniker-makers are of the letters S, E, and X.

Mustang and Cougar, Firebird and Fury, Electra and Riviera—all evocative, and all taken. After World War II, American car buyers had fifty-five individual models on their shopping lists; today, they have almost three hundred. Car namers find it easier to conjure up letters than to comb a thesaurus. It's less expensive, too, given the cost of research, customer clinics, trademark issues, and global retailing. The use of letters also helps manufacturers steer clear of unwanted meanings. Buick was caught in the act when it learned French-Canadians would associate the term "LaCrosse" not with a new sedan, but with slang for, um, self-gratification. The Canadian LaCrosse became the Allure.

Some automakers still believe in the power of a name. What's more appropriate to gung-ho Jeep than a model called the Patriot? Others gamely invent their own names. Picture Volkswagen's harried naming team, under deadline and out of ideas, relieving late-night tension with a stein or three and becoming convinced that combining "tiger" with "leguan"—the German word for "iguana"—was *wunderbar* for its new SUV. It may not have come about quite that way, but VW dealers are now selling something called the Tiguan.

Q Why the hell is Goofy named Goofy?

A In the classic 1980s coming-of-age film *Stand by Me,* a young character named Gordie asks, "Mickey's a mouse, Donald's a duck, Pluto's a dog, what's Goofy?" Given the bizarre pantheon of Disney characters, precisely what Goofy is may not be as easy to identify as how he got his name.

At first blush, you might conclude that "Goofy" is a silly-sounding, made-up word that eventually drew its meaning from the character it first described. Such words are known as eponyms. It's like referring to the toilet as a crapper, after nineteenth-century plumber Thomas Crapper, or calling the act of blasting a friend in the face with a shotgun a "Cheney."

A little etymological sleuthing dismantles this theory. The *Oxford English Dictionary* says "goofy"—meaning "silly" or "daft"—first appeared in print in a February 1921 issue of *Collier's* magazine. That was well before the character we came to know as Goofy made his debut as a member of the audience in the 1932 Disney animated film *Mickey's Revue.*

For his first few years, Goofy didn't even have a name. When he got one in the mid-1930s, it was something goofier than Goofy:

Dippy Dawg. (Spelling "dog" as "dawg" was apparently considered zany in the 1930s.) It was changed in 1938 to Dippy the Goof. By 1939, the Dippy part was gone.

Marching forward under his new name, Goofy starred in nearly fifty Disney cartoons in the 1940s and '50s before going into semi-retirement. (He made a brief and unremarkable comeback in the dismal 1990s television series *The Goof Troop*.)

As for Gordie's question—"What's Goofy?"—the Walt Disney Company states, matter-of-factly, that Goofy is a human character. We'll have to take Disney at its word about that.

Q Why would Jack jump over a candlestick?

Jack be nimble,
Jack be quick.
Jack jump over the candlestick.

A Nursery rhymes, when you think about them, often make little sense. It's hard to picture a cow jumping over the moon, for instance. Nor can we picture someone wearing silver bells or cockle shells. And no matter how we rack our brains, we can't imagine a scenario that requires anyone to jump over a candlestick.

Jumping over a candlestick might be grounds for institutionalization nowadays, but "candle leaping" was once a popular pastime. Back in the days before television, video games, and online poker, people had to invent their own fun. The games that medieval folks concocted weren't always particularly inspired—one popular event at local fairs involved jumping over roaring fires. Eventually, the pain of third-degree burns outweighed whatever fun was to be had with the "game," and bonfires were replaced by candles.

By the seventeenth century, the custom of candle leaping had become associated with November 25, the feast day of Saint Catherine, as a way of foretelling the coming year's events. Candle-jumpers who were lucky enough to clear the candlestick without putting out the flame were supposedly guaranteed good fortune for the year ahead, and those who extinguished the flame were apparently doomed to rotten luck (and scorched feet). How this tradition honored Saint Catherine is not clear, particularly considering that she is the patron saint of educators and students, who should know better.

Indeed, it would have been more logical if the practice was confined to December 27, the feast day of Saint John the Apostle. He is, after all, the patron saint of burns.

Q Does anyone get a parachute on a commercial airplane?

A Commercial airline spokespeople and former pilots will tell you that parachutes are not used on commercial flights. One key reason is that commercial planes fly too high. Parachute jumps are made from between ten thousand and fourteen thousand feet above Earth's surface; commercial airplanes fly between thirty thousand and forty thousand feet up. At that height, a parachutist could freeze, suffer hypoxia (lack of oxygen), and lose consciousness, or be sent into free-fall by air currents that are too strong for the chute to tame.

And even if you waited until the falling plane was within parachuting distance of the ground, you could be injured by falling debris or get caught in some part of the plane. Furthermore, the cabin is pressurized—once the door was opened, you could be sucked out so quickly that you wouldn't have time to get your chute on. On top of all that, most airplane accidents occur on or near the ground, during takeoff or landing; so again, a parachute would prove useless.

Nevertheless, the parachute idea had had proponents. In 2003, inventor Pete Hilsenbeck patented a parachute that could be attached to the back of a passenger seat and be used for bailing out of a disabled plane. But his invention got a swift thumbs-down from aviation ace Guy Norris, then an editor for the respected aerospace weekly publication *Flight International*. "It's got sheer terror written all over it," he told the *New York Times*.

In the 1990s, Robert Nelson, chairman of Ballistic Recovery Systems (BRS), developed a super-size parachute that is strong enough to hold four thousand pounds aloft—the weight of a small plane. The parachute is stored in the rear of the plane and is attached to the plane's wings, nose, and tail with ultra-thin, high-strength wire. In an emergency, it can be fired through the rear window by a miniature rocket. Once outside, it deploys like a huge umbrella and brings the craft to a safe landing. How well does it work? In 2004, Albert Kolk lost control of his small plane while flying over British Columbia. He fired off his BRS parachute, and seconds later, he was gliding, uninjured, to Earth.

NASA officials were so impressed with Nelson's chute that they awarded him a grant to develop one for commercial jets. "Weight and speed are always the challenge," Nelson says. Commercial jets weigh tens of thousands of pounds and travel at speeds of more than six hundred miles per hour.

As of 2009, a parachute capable of supporting a commercial plane had yet to be perfected. But at some point, there might be one aboard every aircraft, enabling pilots to land a disabled plane not just on a wing and a prayer, but with a parachute, too.

Q Why do the British avoid using the letter z?

A The British don't avoid the letter z—Americans just use it a lot more. And it's all because of a guy named Noah Webster.

The American convention is to spell words like "organize" and "idolize" with a z. The common belief is that the British rule is to spell the same words with an s (i.e. "organise" and "idolise"). Examples such as these have led to the notion that the Brits avoid z. And it's easy to see other ways that someone could get the idea—English protests of the letter z (or "zed," as they call it) go back at least to Shakespeare, who wrote in *King Lear*, "Thou whoreson Zed! Thou unnecessary letter!"

But back to America. When Noah Webster began work on his dictionary around the turn of the nineteenth century, he had a number of goals in mind. Of course, he wanted to tell people what words meant. But he also sought to change the way people used the language, especially the ways they spelled words. He wanted American spelling to reflect the virtues of the new republic: honesty, straightforwardness, and an aversion to the unnecessary entanglements of complicated spellings. One of his choices was to use "-ize" and not "-ise" (both were considered correct prior to his standardization).

Many of Webster's alterations—including this one—caught on in America. There's a twist to this tale, though. According to the editors of the *Oxford English Dictionary,* British English has always acknowledged both spellings. The *OED* itself prefers "-ize" because it's closer to the Greek suffix "-izo," from which it derives. Furthermore, the *Encyclopedia Britannica* has always used "-ize," even going back to when this reference work was produced in the British Isles. But in the years since Webster's standardization of American English, "-ise" has become more popular in Britain and Australia—perhaps as a reaction against the American practice.

The tricky part of this whole equation is that some words must be spelled with the "-ise," even in the United States. Unlike words with Greek roots, those with Latin roots that end in "-ise"—such as "incise," "surprise," or "compromise"—can't be tricked out with a z. American patriotism, it seems, has its limits.

Q Did pens once have bladders?

A After the demise of goose-feather quills, which were used for a thousand years, and before the introduction of the ballpoint in 1945, pens did indeed have bladders. Fountain pens were once the writing instruments of choice throughout the world (ask your granddad), and the flexible sac that held the ink was called a bladder. And in the early days, it really *was* a bladder.

Quills had to be dipped in ink frequently. No one could figure out a way to hold the ink above the pen point and make it drip down slowly; it just didn't work. Steel and gold nibs were devised and fitted onto quills and metal writing instruments, but they still had to be dipped into an ink bottle every other word.

In 1819, John Scheffer patented the Penographic, which used part of a pig's bladder attached to a piece of quill. The quill was fitted into a metal tube with a nib at one end. Ink was forced to flow when a lever outside of the tube was pressed; the lever, in turn, pushed on the bladder. The Penographic didn't work particularly well. Other nineteenth-century pens used pistons and rods or buttons to deliver the ink, and some added sponges between the bladder and nib. These weren't efficient, either.

In the 1880s, pen makers realized that the problem was air flow: Ink didn't move smoothly from the bladder to the nib because a vacuum held it back. Lewis E. Waterman, an insurance agent who'd lost a sale when ink spilled all over a contract that a customer was about to sign, recorded a patent for a new pen design. Waterman fashioned a small air channel that ran from the nib to the bladder; the channel allowed an even amount of ink to flow the other way, breaking the vacuum.

Waterman and others began mass-producing their fountain pens. Some were quite fancy, and if you're lucky enough to own one, it could be worth big bucks. Collectors still call the rubberized ink sacs in these pens "bladders," but actual pig bladders have not been used for more than a century. By the 1960s, cartridges replaced ink sacs in most fountain pens, but bladders of all sizes are still sold to pen collectors.

Q Can anyone buy a Popemobile?

A The pope has it pretty sweet. He sits on a golden throne in a golden palace in the center of his very own city-state. Everywhere he goes, millions of people weep and cheer at the mere sight of him. He's so revered that he can get away with wearing a hat that would get the average guy's ass kicked. But perhaps the sweetest perk of the job is the papal set of wheels, better known as the Popemobile.

For most of the history of Christianity, the pope has been treated like royalty—and transported like royalty, too. For hundreds of years, the pope traveled in a gilded papal carriage. After the advent of automobiles, he began traveling in custom-made vehicles that often included open-air platforms from which he could wave to his beseeching subjects.

After a Turkish gunman shot and wounded John Paul II in 1981, bulletproof glass was installed around the platform. It was around then that the term "Popemobile" came into vogue. (Pope John Paul II requested that people refrain from using the term, believing it undignified. Undignified? Come on, buddy—you're riding in a phone booth.)

Many automakers have produced custom vehicles for the pontiff over the years, though Mercedes-Benz has traditionally built the cars that are used at the Vatican. The pope maintains a fleet of vehicles in the papal garage, but when he globe-trots, he doesn't always have to bring his cars with him. Sometimes, Popemobiles are produced for a single papal visit, as with the one that was designed and built by Francisco Motors in 1995 for John Paul II's visit to the Philippines.

What happens to these vehicles after they have served their purpose? And, more importantly, how can we get one? Theoretically, anyone with enough cash and misplaced desire can pay a car company to custom-produce a Popemobile, but good luck trying to get one that has been retired from service. These vehicles are usually displayed as museum pieces. An exception was the Range Rover that was specially produced for the pope's visit to Scotland in 1982. The twenty-four ton, six-wheel vehicle was put up for auction in 2006 and fetched $70,500.

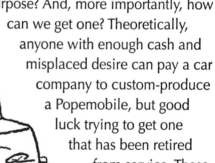

Sometimes, though, you can find other types of cars that have been used by his holiness. In 2005, a German man sold a pope-related vehicle for about 189,000 euros—almost a quarter of a million dollars—on eBay. It was a Volkswagen Golf that Pope Benedict XVI had driven when he was a cardinal. But that's nothing compared to the $690,000 that a Texas lawyer ponied up for one of John Paul II's old cars at a 2005 auction. What was it? A dented, powder-blue 1975 Ford Escort.

Q Why are Persian rugs so expensive?

A If you think that Persian rugs are expensive because they can fly, brace yourself for some bad news: They have no magical qualities. But this doesn't mean they aren't valuable.

Persian is to rugs what Fabergé is to eggs: The term itself implies an expensive, well-crafted item. The Persian rug's reputation for being the best of the best goes back more than a thousand years. Persian rugs are regarded as unique works of art, and because of the amount of knotting involved, they are extremely durable.

What does it take for a carpet to be a Persian rug? For starters, it has to come from Persia, which is otherwise known as Iran. (Iran was known as Persia to the Western world until 1935, when the country requested that it be called Iran. In 1959, it relented and said that either name was permissible. Today, Iranian artistry is called Persian, but the country, in a global political context, is referred to as Iran.)

Carpet weaving is an important aspect of Persian art and culture; it's estimated that weaving is the occupation of one of every seven Iranians. The rugs are made by hand, knot by knot, and are noted for their intricate and colorful designs. Persian adornments often have curved patterns, which are more difficult and time-consuming to create than geometric ones. It can take months or even years to finish a rug.

The value of a Persian rug depends on a variety of factors. The material that is used is one—luxurious silk is more expensive than cotton. In some designs, precious metals such as silver and gold are incorporated. The complexity of the knotting and the design also play a role. Some designs have up to a thousand knots per square inch. Age is important, too. You'll spend a lot more on a rug that's hundreds of years old than on one that's new.

Rugs from the Safavid Dynasty (1502–1736) represent the height of Persian quality. In June 2008, Christie's auction house sold a Persian rug from the Safavid Dynasty for $4.45 million. It doesn't fly, but it's still a helluva rug.

Q Does it cost more to make a penny than a penny is worth?

A When someone offers a penny for your thoughts, you may want to ask for more. In late 2007, the United States Mint reported that its cost to make a penny was 1.67 cents (7.4 billion were minted that year); in May 2008, the cost had dropped to 1.26 cents. At either rate, U.S. taxpayers were not getting their money's worth.

The production cost of a penny includes materials, labor, processing, and transportation. And these expenses don't adversely impact only the penny. Nickels also are worth less than their cost to produce—making a five-cent piece runs nearly ten cents.

In 1792, the newly created U.S. Mint introduced the penny as an all-copper coin; since 1857, it has been an alloy of copper and other metals, typically zinc. With copper prices on the rise, Congress voted in 1982 to change the coin's composition to 97.6 percent zinc core and 2.4 percent copper plating. This made economic sense in 2005, when it cost 0.97 cent to make a penny. But zinc and copper prices increased after that, sending penny production prices soaring beyond a penny.

Some people believe that the penny has outlived its usefulness and should be retired, but it is more likely that Congress instead would vote to change the penny's composition again. Metal prices fluctuate, and the cost of making coins rises and falls accordingly. (Congress has changed the penny's composition half a dozen times over the years.) So don't look for the penny to disappear anytime soon.

Q Did black artists perform in black-face minstrel shows?

A Before the Civil War: hardly ever. After the Civil War: frequently.

Minstrel shows were ensemble performances in which all the men on stage darkened their faces with burnt cork and joked around as if they were black—even though they were not. For years, the performers were white, and so were the audiences.

Minstrel shows began in the early nineteenth century, when the enslavement of blacks was a reality in America. All the songs, dances, and jokes were based on ugly stereotypes of black slaves or of free blacks.

Few black ensembles performed in these early shows, and only one black man toured with white entertainers: William Henry Lane, or "Master Juba." Lane grew up in New York City and was the best jig dancer in the city; some consider him the first tap dancer. He toured with a minstrel group called the Ethiopian Serenaders. Lane died in London in the 1850s, while still a young man.

Minstrel shows enjoyed incredible popularity, but they almost disappeared during the American Civil War. After 1865, with the war over, minstrels again drew big audiences—but with a significant difference: Shows with all-black casts began touring. The performers used the same burnt-cork makeup, silly dances, and demeaning jokes as the white groups.

Why would black men make fun of their own race this way? Sadly, it was often the only paying job available to black entertainers. For example, Broadway star Bert Williams and blues musician W. C. Handy worked in minstrel shows before becoming famous. For them, and many other black performers, it was a way to get on stage, advance their careers, and pay the bills.

CONTRIBUTORS

Vickey Kalambakal is a writer and historian based in Southern California. She writes for textbooks, encyclopedias, magazines, and ezines.

Jack Greer is a writer living in Chicago.

Diane Lanzillotta Bobis is a food, fashion, and lifestyle writer from Glenview, Illinois.

Anthony G. Craine is a contributor to the *Britannica Book of the Year* and has written for magazines including *Inside Sports* and *Ask*. He is a former United Press International bureau chief.

Pat Sherman is a writer living in Cambridge, Massachusetts. She is the author of several books for children, including *The Sun's Daughter* and *Ben and the Proclamation of Emancipation*.

Brett Kyle is a writer living in Draycott, Somerset, England. He is also an actor, musician, singer, and playwright.

Joshua D. Boeringa is a writer living in Mt. Pleasant, Michigan. He has written for magazines and Web sites.

Tom Harris is a Web project consultant, editor, and writer living in Atlanta. He is the co-founder of Explainist.com, and was leader of the editorial content team at HowStuffWorks.com.

Letty Livingston is a dating coach, relationship counselor, and sexpert. Her advice column, Let Letty Help, has been published

in more than forty periodicals and on the Internet (letlettyhelp.
blogspot.com).

Carrie Williford is a writer living in Atlanta. She was a contributing
writer to HowStuffWorks.com.

Noah Liberman is a Chicago-based sports, entertainment, and business writer who has published two books and has contributed
articles to a wide range of newspapers and national magazines.

Alex Nechas is a writer and editor based in Chicago.

Jessica Royer Ocken is a freelance writer and editor based in
Chicago.

Brett Ballantini is a sportswriter who has written for several major
sports teams and has authored a book titled *The Wit and Wisdom
of Ozzie Guillen*.

Shanna Freeman is a writer and editor living near Atlanta. She also
works in an academic library.

Chuck Giametta is a highly acclaimed journalist who specializes
in coverage of the automotive industry. He has written and edited
books, magazines, and Web articles on many automotive topics.

ArLynn Leiber Presser is a writer living in suburban Chicago. She is
the author of twenty-seven books.

Angelique Anacleto specializes in style and beauty writing. She
has written for salon industry publications and has authored a
children's book.

Thad Plumley is an award-winning writer who lives in Dublin, Ohio. He is the director of publications and information products for the National Ground Water Association.

Paul Forrester is a writer and editor who lives in New York City.

Dan Dalton is a writer and editor living in the Pacific Northwest.

Jeff Moores is an illustrator whose work appears in periodicals and advertisements, and as licensed characters on clothing. Visit his Web site (jeffmoores.com) to see more of his work.

Factual verification: Darcy Chadwick, Barbara Cross, Bonny M. Davidson, Andrew Garrett, Cindy Hangartner, Brenda McLean, Carl Miller, Katrina O'Brien, Marilyn Perlberg